Find Your Confidence

The no-nonsense guide to self-belief

Holly Matthews

GREEN TREE

LONDON • OXFORD • NEW YORK • NEW DELHI • SYDNEY

GREEN TREE
Bloomsbury Publishing Plc
50 Bedford Square, London, WC1B 3DP, UK
29 Earlsfort Terrace, Dublin 2, Ireland

BLOOMSBURY, GREEN TREE and the Green Tree logo are trademarks of Bloomsbury
Publishing Plc

First published in Great Britain 2024

A catalogue record for this book is available from the British Library.

Library of Congress Cataloguing-in-Publication data has been applied for.

ISBN: TPB: 978-1-3994-0934-6; eBook: 978-1-3994-0933-9; ePdf: 978-1-3994-0935-3

2 4 6 8 10 9 7 5 3 1

Text design by Austin Taylor
Typeset in Aestetico by Deanta Global Publishing Services, Chennai, India
Printed and bound in Great Britain by CPI Group (UK) Ltd., Croydon, CR0 4YY

To find out more about our authors and books visit www.bloomsbury.com and sign up
for our newsletters.

Dedicated to my two main girls, Brooke and Texas.
It's all for you, my darlings.

Contents

Introduction

I have a secret that I'm going to share.

This may be a surprise, given the nature of the book, and it's something that might surprise even those closest to me. So gather round and huddle in:

I am not *always* confident. I do not *always* have belief in myself.

In fact, I've had many 'confidence dips' in my life. However, after trial and error, and lots of lessons learned from giving life a good go, I have developed systems and structures to put in place to support myself whenever I do experience these dips.

You will too.

You see, everyone is born with confidence. As a teeny tiny baby, you demanded with gusto that your needs be met and your first words were uttered without embarrassment. Maybe we forget this fact and maybe that confidence gets rocked from time to time, but the truth remains the same: inside you, running through you (like the writing in a stick of Blackpool rock) is a confident and self-assured badass. We just sometimes need to remind ourselves of this and find our confidence again.

Now, when we think of confidence and what it actually means, it will likely bring up different things for different people. Maybe you think confidence is delivering a flawless presentation at work or having the ability to be charismatic and witty while talking to someone you fancy. You might see confidence as the ability to set clear boundaries in your life or stand up for yourself with friends. How we define what confidence is can be very personal. When you think of a confident person, what do you see? Take a moment to think about this now.

The origin of the word confidence is the Latin word *fidere*, which means 'to trust'. Confidence therefore is 'to trust'; to have faith in something (often before we know factually whether it can be done).

'**Confidence** is not a state that is set in stone – it's **absolutely something we can work on.**'

Self-confidence is something we may find we skate in and out of during our lifetimes or even in different areas of our lives. Perhaps you are a very confident parent but stick you in a work setting and you crumble. Or perhaps you might thrive in social situations but struggle to feel good when looking in the mirror. Confidence is not a state that is set in stone and it's absolutely something we can work on.

It's also worth noting that a lack of confidence and self-belief can sneak up on us over time. Perhaps you once did see yourself as confident and suddenly you've noticed that you don't speak up in social settings any more or that you wouldn't dream of wearing anything but black or grey (yet you used to head to the chip shop dressed like a pageant queen).

Maybe you used to be the Chatty Cathy at any event but years of living with a critical partner has chipped away at your self-worth and now just popping to the supermarket feels daunting. The eroding of the belief that you 'can' may take years to develop, but it really doesn't need to take years to unpick. That's where I come in.

I chose to write about confidence and self-belief because when you unlock this within yourself, life just becomes that bit easier. Having confidence will help you to have more connected relationships, a brighter outlook and, ultimately, a trust that even when things are tough YOU are going to work it out.

I chose to write about confidence because for so many people whom I work with, it's their lack of self-belief that is holding them back more than anything else in life. When they realise that they have the ability to work on their confidence and build it up like a muscle, it frees them up and we start to see positive change. I want that for you too.

In this book, I'm going to take your hand and guide you through some of life's testing moments. We are going to work together as a team to help you find your confidence. I promise I won't chuck you in at the deep end but I will certainly be making you jump in at points (with some armbands on at first). I will share with you the tools and ideas that will help you steer yourself through the chaos of being an adult, with poise and conviction and, of course, with confidence.

Why me?

Before we go any further, I'd like to offer a quick introduction to who I am (I probably should have begun with this, but I was eager to get started!). I am Holly, the woman who will be chatting to you throughout this book and someone who is utterly obsessed with you living a life that feels great to you.

I am a qualified NLP (neuro-linguistic programming) practitioner, life coach (although I prefer the name self-development coach, as it sounds less like I'm telling you how to live your life), intuitive psychology coach, hypnotherapist, former TV actress (who still dabbles in telly now and then) and mum to two awesome daughters, Brooke and Texas.

I am also the founder of The Happy Me Project, which is a community that consists of in-person events, a podcast, books and an online self-development membership. I will reference my membership throughout this book as it has become such an incredible community of like-minded people (for those who'd like to know a bit more, skip to p. 271, where I've put all the details).

Alongside my on-paper experience I also happen to be a human who has been through a whole heap of tough stuff (who hasn't, right?). Following the death of my brilliant husband, Ross, to brain cancer in 2017, I immersed myself further in self-development.

After Ross's death it became way more important to me to find ways to help us all live a life that feels great. I (and all of Ross's loved ones) got chucked this massive painful reminder that life is short, and for me it also came with a drive to help people unlock what might be holding them back from living their lives to the fullest.

I have gone back through my history and revisited times when I made choices that didn't always support me, and I have been able to notice both what works and what doesn't. Embracing my flaws and laughing at my chaos has also helped me to foster more compassion for myself and find a confidence outside of the partnership that Ross and I shared.

I gave more details of Ross's death and the impact of this in my first book, *The Happy Me Project: The no-nonsense guide to self-development* (2022), but I will most definitely be sharing more of my personal anecdotes within this one too, all mixed in with a good dollop of scientific research, stories from my clients and tips from other experts.

Housekeeping note: I have put all links to any research references on my website – www.iamhollymatthews.com/findyourconfidence – so as not to make this book the length of *War and Peace*.

How to use this book

Since we're all so different from each other and need different levels of support in different aspects of our lives (and at different times of our lives), each of the nine chapters will focus on boosting our confidence in a different common everyday scenario. We'll be looking at: public speaking, social situations, standing up for yourself, starting something new, the workplace, relationships, parenting, job interviews and your appearance.

A reminder though that this is *your* book and I want you to read it in a way that feels right for you. Some of you more traditional readers will work from front to back in an orderly fashion, while others might prefer to head straight to the chapter that focuses on your personal area of difficulty. It's your choice. Jump in and feel free to use the book as you like: write in it, highlight your favourite bits and even fold those pages (I dare ya!).

Each chapter is divided into mini segments and packed with practical tips for you to play around with throughout. Each one ends with a selection of activities to bring everything together. These are split into work for the 'internal self' (how I feel on the inside) and the 'external self' (how I look on the outside).

Although the majority of our work will focus on the internal stuff, I wanted to include aspects of how we can look and present more confidently too. As a former TV actress, I am a professional pretender and so I'm well versed in this area; when instructed, I can act sad, scared, excited or like a confident woman who knows her worth. I'm the perfect person to share with you the skills to 'fake it till you make it'.

I appreciate that the 'fake it till you make it' method is a controversial one because often people assume it means 'fake it' without doing the deeper work on your internal self-development, too. But not here! Together, we're going to combine the two and recognise that the internal work and the external work sit side by side and impact each other, so the 'fake it till you make it' approach works as long as we're using it as a means of topping up the important internal stuff, and not on its own. If you're dubious about the external approach, let me share a quick example of what I mean.

One way actors find the emotion of a character is via their physical selves. If I were to play a sad and nervous character, for example, I could naturally begin to make myself look less confident by simply adopting a posture where my body was slumped, my shoulders rolled forward and my eyes avoided anyone's gaze. This unconfident pose can start to impact my internal world too.

Give it a try yourself now: begin with your shoulders back, your chin up and a broad smile and then shift to having your eyes down, shoulders forward, arms folded around your body and no smile on your face.

Feel the difference?

There will be descriptions of different body language techniques you can try throughout the book. Since this can sometimes be a tad more challenging to describe, I've put some extra visuals for you on my website too, if needed: https://www.iamhollymatthews.com/findyourconfidence/.

Given that I'm introducing myself, now is probably a good time to tell you that my brain is not neurotypical and I am a human with ADHD. I reference this at various points in the book and it means that I fully appreciate anything bite-size and chunked down, which lends itself very well to sharing tips with you, so I've structured the book in this way.

A huge caveat here, too, is that this book is in no way a replacement for therapy. I am not a doctor – I am a coach – and I am a huge believer in therapy in all its forms. This book can, however, sit alongside your therapy work (you can even share your thoughts *with* your therapist after reading this book) and if you've been thinking about reaching out to a counsellor or psychiatrist, this is your nudge to go do so (*see* 'Other resources' on p. 270 if you'd like some ideas on where to begin.).

Before we begin...

As with all my work, I want to make it clear from the outset that I'm not asking you to put any pressure on yourself when reading this book (there's enough pressure in the world at large, right?). So please be kind to yourself. This is all about helping you to feel better.

Let's throw perfection out of the window and first recognise that if you've picked this book up then it's already a huge win. The likelihood is that you want to feel more confident and build your self-esteem, so buying this book is the first brave step in doing this work.

I won't ram concepts down your throat as some gospel truth, but we will be talking through many different ideas that lots of people before us have found beneficial (and so perhaps you will too). Some of the things we'll discuss you will discover that you like and others you may prefer to discard, but I'm confident you'll find what you need.

Choose ideas that speak to you to create your own personal action plan. You are unique and so your route to true self-belief will be as individual as your fingerprints (and I'll be here throughout, cheering loudly, whatever you decide!). Wherever you are with your confidence at the moment, you are at the perfect place to start, and I'm so glad you're here.

If any of you are already doubting yourself and convinced that this won't work for you, then I am here to call BS (with total love and support chucked in, of course). I know that if you approach this book with a willingness to learn and a student mindset – imagine it's your first day of school, if you will – then change and confidence are firmly within your grasp. I know this because I have had the pleasure of watching many of my clients turn into their most confident selves, so I know this is absolutely possible for you too.

A promise

Before we head on into the meat and bones of this book, I want to get a little commitment out of you. This isn't for me, it's for you. It's some accountability, a little nudge in the right direction, a commitment to yourself. You're here for positive change and to make your life feel great. So, let's start by you saying this promise to yourself, either in your head or out loud if possible.

(I feel like we should be standing or doing something symbolic right now, such as holding our hands on our hearts or looking wistfully into the distance. Although perhaps that's a bit dramatic, in which case perhaps just try to shut the door on your noisy family for 10 minutes so you can focus as you read the following…)

I promise myself that I will read this book with an open mind.
I promise myself that I will read at least some of this book.
I promise myself that I will have a go at some action steps I read in the book.
I promise that I will be kind to myself when I feel challenged, triggered or it seems hard.
I promise myself that I will let go of old stories and be willing to make new, empowering ones.
I promise that I will give myself permission to step into this new confident version of me.

Once you have said this to yourself (you may even want to write it down or snap a picture of the promise as a reminder) take a nice full breath in and a lovely big sigh out. Then let's get to work!

Holly x

#1

Public speaking

At around the age of 18 I was a guest at a friend's wedding. I knew a few people there and the best man was a good friend of my then boyfriend. They were all from a pretty small town in Cumbria, and this meant that a big chunk of the town was there on the day.

We took our seats for the speeches and, as the room silenced, the best man stood up to do his obligatory speech. All eyes were on him and each ticking second that he *didn't* speak felt like an eternity.

One second, two seconds, three seconds…

You could have heard a pin drop as his body language leaked his discomfort and a few people began to shift in their seats or clear their throats.

Four seconds, five seconds, six seconds…

He eventually began. 'I … erm … I' and then once more he went quiet and looked at his feet, while gripping a crumpled bit of paper in his hands. You could almost hear his heartbeat thumping in his chest, along with the collective awkwardness of the audience, who were quite literally holding their breath.

As a performer, I felt sick for him. I knew the stage fright he was living from personal experience, and I wanted to run up there and help him out. He opened his mouth to speak once more and said, 'I've, oh god, I'm so sorry, I've bottled it, I can't do it' to a stunned room.

Thankfully, the father of the bride took the wheel and allowed the best man to sit down (or slump down, which is what actually happened) and the rest of us breathed a sigh of relief that the ordeal we had all been part of was finally over.

It's been about 20 years since I witnessed this scene and it's stayed with me because I hated how stuck that man felt in the moment. I hated knowing that he would have felt he had let himself down and let his friends down, and I have always wondered if he ever did anything like that again or if he conquered his fear of public speaking. I guess I'll never know, but one thing is for sure: I don't want anyone to *ever* feel so suffocated by speaking up. So, in this chapter, I'm going to share the wisdom, the science and the tools that I really wanted to give to that terrified best man on that day.

Why are we so scared of speaking in public?

A 2015 study at the Chapman University in California looked at 'fears of the average American' and discovered that 30 per cent of Americans felt 'afraid' or 'very afraid' of public speaking. This meant that public speaking was ranked by the test subjects as scarier than hurricanes, earthquakes, floods or even dying. (My non-scientific guess is that a number of you reading this now are nodding along with agreement at these results.)

The fear of public speaking is called glossophobia and, like most of our human behaviour, experts believe there is an evolutionary reason behind it.

Essentially, in the distant past, humans would have been at threat from large predators and so evolved to operate in groups for safety. (This makes sense because a lone human isn't going to scare off a predator, but a group of people might.) Therefore, historically, humans' ability to work collaboratively in a group, to keep an eye out for one another and to defend each other, was needed for our survival. Back in the cave-painting days, if a human was pushed out on their own, out of the group, that ostracism would have probably meant they'd be dead meat very soon after. Public speaking – standing out alone – goes against this group mentality.

There is also the idea that during these prehistoric times, having eyes facing towards you (as happens when standing in front of an audience for public speaking) probably meant we were being watched by a predator. Our bodies would then have responded in the way they do in times of danger.

When we face a threat, perceived or otherwise, a signal is sent to the amygdala, which sits in the temporal lobe of the brain. When the amygdala receives this signal, it immediately sounds the alarm throughout the body to activate the fight, flight, freeze response. The adrenal glands (located on top of the kidneys) receive the signal to dump adrenaline into the blood, which begins the fight-or-flight feeling as the heart rate increases, blood pressure rises and the brain begins to receive more oxygen. The body is preparing to fight for its survival. This response happens instantly and without you needing to do anything.

Let us remind ourselves that although we feel far removed from our primitive ancestors, it wasn't *that* long ago in terms of human existence (the Neolithic or New Stone Age was roughly 6000 years ago), and evolution and our brains may still be responding to the primordial fears we've just discussed. So, let's be kind to ourselves – there's a lot going on under the surface!

It's worth noting, of course, that if you ask most people why they fear public speaking, evolutionary factors would certainly not be their answer. They would likely cite a previous bad experience of speaking in front of others or their fear of other people judging them. They would talk about their worry of messing up, making mistakes and looking stupid in front of an audience.

I'm going to share my own anecdotal 'looking stupid while public speaking' story because we're all friends here. This story takes us back to 10-year-old me standing up in front of the whole school during assembly. I have always loved the idea of giving back and at this time in my life I had spent my weekend selling to the neighbours on my street (and there's no better way of phrasing this than…) 'bits of crap' I had found around the house or had made. I'd made a profit of £15 and was very proud to announce that I was donating this money to the Marie Curie cancer charity.

The headmistress of the school, Ms Curd, asked me up on stage and I stood proudly in front of my peers to explain what I had been up to. I chatted confidently about my 'shop' and how much I'd raised for charity. She then asked me which charity I was donating the money to and I stated, with the same confidence and vigour as before, that my donation was going to … 'the Mariah Curry charity' (clearly a mix of one of my favourite artists and one of my favourite foods!). As laughter filled the room and my face flushed red, I thought, 'What have I said wrong, why are they laughing?' I sheepishly took my seat as I heard Ms Curd chuckle the correct name, 'Marie Curie'. I felt so embarrassed.

I think about that moment every time I see anything to do with the Marie Curie charity, even to this day. This is the unfortunate power of embarrassing public speaking moments: they can create a limiting belief about public speaking in our subconscious minds. Even if we aren't aware of these subconscious limiting beliefs forming, they can mean that our brains will instantly associate any new public speaking opportunities with the old negative ones. These limiting beliefs can be hard to shift.

You might imagine that with my background as an actress, standing up and talking in public would come easy to me. But for years I was highly confident when portraying a character on stage, but the idea of speaking as myself in public would have been as abhorrent to me as fighting a lion is to most sensible people. I had the fear and I had to learn how to just be me without the mask of a character. I discovered there was a major reason for my fear...

I struggled with public speaking because I kept telling myself that I wasn't good at public speaking.

What you say creates the way

Think back to the last time you had to do any kind of speaking in public. This doesn't have to be an actual speech – perhaps you had to run a training session with your team or do one of those awkward introductions at a new class or event. You know the type – 'Tell us a "fun" fact about yourself or what is your favourite food' – and in that moment you decide there's *nothing* fun about you at all, and trying to come up with *any* food will have you stuttering 'table' because thoughts and words seem to have evaded you completely.

Do you have an example in mind? Are you starting to sweat just bringing back the memory?

OK, first, take a breath. It's not happening now. You are safe and sound reading a book. Second, I want you to think about the moments *before* you did the public speaking and consider your internal self then. What were you saying to yourself? Can you remember? Maybe you can or maybe you can hazard a guess...

Essentially, I'd like you to consider whether you were giving yourself a cheerleading-style motivational talk before your public speaking or whether you were scolding yourself and focusing your mind on past negative experiences and the anxiety that came with them.

I'm going to be bold here (when am I not?) and say that if you feel scared about public speaking then I'm guessing you were fairly certainly doing the latter. Why am I asking this?

Well, what we say can shape the way we do things, both positively and negatively. So, in the context of public speaking, if we keep telling ourselves that we aren't the type of person who does public speaking, our brains take that as an instruction and accept it as fact.

I asked people in The Happy Me Project community to describe what it feels like to do any kind of public speaking, and if they thought they were good at it. I was told:

- 'I'm terrible. It's cringe and my mouth goes dry.'
- 'I shake, my heart beats fast and I'm awful.'
- 'I get so scared that I forget all my words.'

There were, of course, *some* positive responses, but a huge majority told me how bad they were at doing public speaking and how they actively avoid it.

Using critical language to describe ourselves, such as the above, leads to us feeling fear, shame and anxiety, and can likely result in inaction. No good ever comes from negative self-talk, even though many of my clients have told me they assumed it would 'motivate' them.

Moment to pause

Let's stop to think about this properly. Start by picturing someone you care about; then imagine they were about to speak up at work and do a presentation. Before they get up, you sit beside them and begin to berate them.

'You're terrible at public speaking! Remember that time you introduced the musicians at school and said "penis" instead of "pianist"? Everyone laughed at you, didn't they? And then you went all red and sweaty and couldn't get the rest of the words out. You're going to be *so* bad at this presentation and I bet you'll stutter over your words. In fact, I bet you can't even remember your words, can you? Wow you really are bad at this! Plus, your hair is a mess and your trousers make you look frumpy.'

Now that would be a pretty horrendous thing to do to someone, right? And I know you wouldn't dream of acting in this way. But so many people do this to *themselves* before any kind of public speaking, and then wonder why their confidence begins to dip. Therefore, the negative self-talk has to change to something more compassionate if we want to become a public speaking legend. Considering how we might speak to someone else before they did some public speaking could help us to be in the right ballpark when checking on our own inner dialogue.

In a 2014 study by the American Psychological Association, psychologists looked at the pronouns we use when adopting self-talk and how these can impact how we feel. They noticed that the subtle switch from using the word 'I' in self-talk to the word 'you' or your own name can have a soothing, distancing and self-regulatory effect.

In the study, participants were given just five minutes to prepare a speech (I know, I know, some of you reading this are feeling second-hand panic for the participants in the study, but bear with me…). Some participants were told to talk to themselves before the speech by using the pronoun 'I', while others were told to use the word 'you' or their own name.

> "Negative self-talk has to change to something **more compassionate.**"

The experiment found that the participants who used 'I' said things like: 'Oh, my god, how am I going to do this? I can't prepare a speech in five minutes without notes. It takes days for me to prepare a speech!' These participants were far more critical in their approach.

Those who used their own name or 'you' were much more likely to give themselves advice, support and a motivational pep talk, such as: 'You've got this, Holly; sure, you only have five minutes to prepare but you can do this. Just do your best!'

Essentially, the study concluded that it seemed much easier to be nicer to the 'other' person, even if that other person was actually ourself. So, next time you're due to give a presentation or do some other form of public speaking, try giving yourself a gentle pep talk by switching 'I' for your own name and imagine talking to yourself as if to a best friend. It's amazing what some kind words can do for your confidence.

Don't 'calm down'

What is the first thing that someone will say to you when you're feeling nervous about speaking in public? I think high up on the list will be 'calm down'.

'Calm down' might be the most infuriating piece of advice we can be given before public speaking, when we inevitably feel anything but calm. (So I forgive you, by the way, if you find yourself screeching 'I'm trying to calm down, Susan!' into the affronted face of your 'helpful' friend or colleague when offered this particular piece of advice.)

Harvard professor Alison Wood Brooks looked into whether the 'calm down' strategy actually works when it comes to public speaking. In her extensive studies, in which participants were either performing karaoke or public speaking, Wood Brooks found that those who told themselves to 'calm down' before their performance were rated much lower in terms of the success of their performances. By contrast, those who affirmed 'I'm excited' were considered to have delivered far more engaging performances and were seen as more confident.

What?!

So, here we are, about to step up to deliver a presentation to our bosses about the quarterly metrics (in my mind it's being delivered by Harvey Specter from TV's *Suits*). We're getting ready by saying 'calm down' to ourselves and it's making us look … crap?

The reason for this seems to be because before a performance many of us will naturally have pre-performance nerves or 'performance anxiety', which is a heightened or aroused state. By contrast, the act of being calm is very different because, well, it's calm. So attempting to go from feeling anxious to feeling calm can be too big an emotional jump for most of us to achieve, which makes it fairly ineffective advice.

Feelings of anxiety and excitement, however, feel more similar in the way we experience them in our bodies. This means we can confuse our brains into thinking the anxiety we are feeling is actually excitement. So next time you're about to present, rather than calming yourself down why not try to hype yourself up? 'I'm so excited to share my work on the quarterly metrics' and 'I'm excited to present my work to colleagues to help us move the conservation along.'

This trickery can be a wonderful way to help our brains face what we're doing with a more excited and open approach, which has the added bonus of lowering our anxiety. Give it a go next time you present and see what happens.

Breathe, babe, breathe

I love to find the low-hanging fruit of the self-development world. I appreciate there are times when we really need to go deep, get into it with our therapists and get messy, but there are often simple solutions to our everyday challenges that we overlook.

Breathing is one example. We forget that breathing correctly can be the difference between a stumbling and panicked presentation or a serene and confident one. So let me share with you my top tips when it comes to breathing and public speaking work.

Before public speaking

Breathwork can be used to regulate the nervous system and help us feel more in control before a performance. These are my favourite breathing patterns, which you can try:

4, 7, 8 breathing
Breathe in through the nose for four counts, hold for seven, then breathe out through the mouth forcefully for eight (with a nice 'whoosh' sound added in if you're feeling a bit spicy today). Repeat to complete four rounds.

Box breathing
Breathe in through your nose for four counts, hold for four counts, breathe out of your nose for four counts and then hold for four counts. Repeat as needed.

Alternate nostril breathing

Close your right nostril with your right thumb. Breathe in through your left nostril and then close it with your finger. Release your thumb from your right nostril and breathe out through that side. Breathe in through your right nostril, then close it again with your thumb. Release your finger from your left nostril and breathe out through that side. Repeat as much as feels good.

During your public speaking

Having a focus on our breath as we speak can help bring our attention inwards (and away from those watching eyes). Pausing can also be used effectively in our speech to add weight to a particular point. Experiment with pausing and taking a breath in different places in your speech as you practise beforehand.

After public speaking

There's nothing like the sigh of relief of someone who just nailed their public speaking. And listen, 'nailing it' will be different for everyone. It could be getting through it and simply not running out of the room, or it could mean trying one of the tips we've discussed so far in this chapter for the first time. This is not about comparing yourself to anyone but yourself and doing your best.

So far, we've been discussing the internal work we can do to find our confidence with public speaking, so it's time now to take a look at the work we can do on the outside too.

What does confidence 'look' like in public speaking?

A great speaker will engage us and take us on a journey. They will inspire us, challenge us and perhaps even make us laugh along the way. We know people like this in our personal lives and we see them on stages or on TV too. I bet there is someone in your life right now who can keep you on the edge of your seat with hilarious stories of their latest adventures, their annoying colleagues or their embarrassing dates.

My Grandad Matty, or 'Matt the Cat' as he was known around Newcastle, was a great speaker, and he's who comes to mind for me. He was a union man and was just as comfortable in the murkiest of pubs and clubs in the East End of Newcastle as he was with the upper crust at some fancy political shindig.

We all have friends and family who speak confidently – it doesn't have to be their job. They just know how to yarn a good tale and chat with ease. For us to understand how we can take what some do naturally and learn it for ourselves, it's helpful to not only focus on the internal work we can do to support ourselves, but also to unpick what makes people look confident when speaking, too.

As human beings we are trained to pick up on body language, and in fact 70 per cent of what we read from people comes from their non-verbal signals. In the world of confidence, then, body language is hugely important. We can use this knowledge to our advantage: if people are looking out for certain indicators that signify confidence and we know what these indicators are (which you will, because I'm going to tell you!), we can get ahead with looking at ease while speaking. Let's start by examining one of the big players in the 'looking confident' arena.

Hands

Used effectively, your hands can act as the paintbrush that colours the stories you are telling. They can help your audience (whether it's an audience of 1 or 1000) follow what is being said, and even help you to stay in your own flow of speech. Imagine how dull and odd-looking it would be if people sat on their hands and just spouted words at you. It would seem awkward, wouldn't it? Even if you're not at the top of your game in terms of hand usage I'd imagine you still use your hands a bit. Give it a shot right now: talk while sitting on your hands… Does it feel weird? (Also, if you're sitting on your own doing this, I'm high-fiving you because you are my people!)

The gestures we use as we speak can also help the audience remember things we say. Throw in a clap, a click or a bold hand gesture and whatever you said to accompany it will be way more anchored in their memories than almost anything else you say.

The next time you see a politician on TV, watch their hands. They will use them … a lot! There will be common gestures that are used frequently (can you spot any of these?) and then some that are actively avoided due to their negative connotations, such as pointing.

None of the politician's gestures will be an accident because they are taught this stuff. They use their body language to appear likeable, strong and like the leaders they wish to be. In fact, here in the UK, it was reported that government ministers had been given skills training from the Royal Academy of Dramatic Art (RADA), an elite drama school attended by Anthony Hopkins, Joan Collins and Alan Rickman, to name just a few.

Did these politicians work with RADA because they wanted to be the next Meryl Streep or Denzel Washington? No. (I say that, but perhaps there were a few who had sneaky aspirations of getting their big Hollywood break. I can see it now, *Fast & Furious 352* starring David Cameron, Jeremy Hunt and Vin Diesel.) The politicians in fact took lessons to improve their body language; to look confident and self-assured to their voters.

Just a little note of reassurance here: even though I am giving you lots of ideas in this chapter, I don't expect you to be able to go and do everything immediately. Everyone is different and if you are a total novice when it comes to public speaking then it's all about the baby steps and working on one stage at a time (at a pace that suits you). It's just good to know the options that are out there and where we might progress to as we learn.

So, to get you started, let's look at some hand gestures that you can try (and if you head to my website, I have some visuals to help you with these too, since I appreciate describing body language can be a tad clunky):

Symbolic hand gestures

This might be holding your fingers up to indicate an amount: 'I ate three [hold up three fingers] biscuits today, when I said I would have zero [make a circle with finger and thumb].' Or perhaps we add in a flat palm up in front of us as we say, 'Somebody needs to say "stop" [add the "stop" gesture as you say the word] because Holly is eating all the biscuits!' My example here may or may not be because I have just eaten three Hobnobs...

Descriptive hand gestures

These might look like raising your hand up, fingers slightly bent to indicate height, or holding your first finger and thumb almost touching to indicate something is small.

Emotional hand gestures

The flat palm or two flat palms together held across your heart could indicate pain, love or connection to an emotion. Or the punching of a fist into the palm of the other hand may indicate anger.

Visual aid hand gestures

This can be as simple as pointing at something to indicate where to look, whether that be a whiteboard or another prop you may have, such as a book or painting. A good thing to note here is that, particularly in the Western world, pointing can be seen as aggressive. However, you can soften that aggression by simply not pointing with your finger and instead making your hand into a fist and putting your thumb on top of your first finger. You can then point using the middle knuckle of the first finger and tip of the thumb. Watch any politician get angry in the House of Commons and you'll likely see this exact gesture.

Start to become aware of how you are currently using your hands and have a play around with some of these gestures or notice how many you already use.

Practise and play around

Try practising BIG hand gestures too, because teeny tiny ones can look like teeny tiny levels of confidence. Notice what it feels like to hold your arms straight out at either side of your body, taking up as much space as possible. For some people this can be extremely challenging and might make them feel foolish. Try it and notice at what point it feels too much.

It's also helpful to consider where your hands are in the eyeline of your audience because in terms of how confident we perceive people to be, it does matter. There is a kind of 'golden area' for hand gestures that our eyes see, which is where the diaphragm or the top of the stomach is. If you place your hands in this golden area as you talk then you appear more confident, but if your hands drop below this area then it looks a little odd. I know that for some of you this golden area will feel high up right now and you may need some practice. That's great, though, because when it comes to confidence, practice is the name of the game.

Moving on from our hands, let's shimmy on over to discussing movement more generally.

Movement

When you're asked to give a speech or talk in front of others the last thing you might want to do is move. In fact,

'When it comes to confidence, practice is the name of the game.'

you may have experienced actively freezing up when presenting before. Or, on the other hand, perhaps your nerves got the better of you and you found yourself moving awkwardly around aimlessly or tapping your foot incessantly. Ideally, in order to look our most confident, we don't want to be completely rigid but nor do we want to be pacing around like a cat on a hot tin roof. It's all about hitting that sweet spot in the middle. Let's dig more into what this means in real terms.

In the world of acting, actors are taught only to move if there is a motivation to move. In day-to-day real life, we never just move (e.g. walk across a room) for no reason; it's always motivated by something, for example we might be collecting something or doing something or hugging someone. We can also apply this concept of moving only for a purpose when it comes to public speaking.

Here are some suggestions for naturally incorporating movement into a speaking situation:

- Moving to get a prop or to show something, e.g. moving out of the way so the screen behind you is visible.
- Moving towards a person who has asked a question.
- Moving on a thought or topic change – this could mean moving to the other side of the stage or room, or something far more subtle, such as moving to a new cue card.

And here are some movements to avoid:

- Rocking, swaying or shuffling from foot to foot, since this type of movement implies nervousness.
- Randomly darting across a space without rhyme or reason; as discussed, this feels unnatural and can make you look awkward.

- Oscillating between a laptop and a presentation screen, which is confusing for the audience and can make you appear unprepared.

The ideas I'm suggesting that you try here are fairly mild, and that's on purpose. A big movement-based no-no is trying something too daring that could result in you injuring yourself. I know this might feel like a moot point, but I once watched a woman talk about her story at an empowerment event for women in business (in gory detail) then, after showing clear signs of anxiety throughout, she decided to finish with a high kick (literally!). It ended with her being ambulanced out of the venue.

I'm not saying that you *can't* do a high kick. If you are highly skilled at high kicking and feel fully capable and ready, then you do you (I mean, it's a confident stance to take and that's the whole point of the book). For the rest of us, though, I suggest sticking with movements that make sense in the context, support the points you're making and, most importantly, don't detract from your words.

> "Remind yourself that you don't have to say everything perfectly. **We connect with people** more when there's a **humanness in how they talk.**"

Voice

Whether you have a regional accent or sound like Keira Knightley in *Pride and Prejudice*, your voice is an important tool in being seen as confident. Growing up with a northern accent, I was taught by my equally northern dad to enunciate and slow down when I spoke. He taught me to be confident in my accent and not to feel pressure to lose it. He said that as long as I was conscious of speaking to be understood, then I could speak as I wished. It was sound advice that I still stand by today and I'm passing it on to you too.

Moment to pause

Let's stop and consider the voice for a moment. It's helpful to know your starting point so you can see where any tweaks might be made. How would you describe your voice? Have you ever thought about this before? Is it high, low, raspy, timid, booming? Can you come up with three descriptive words for your voice right now?

Some of you reading this will be squirming as you think about the sound of your voice, after listening back to a voice note or online meeting and hearing what other people hear. Isn't it strange how different we sound to others compared to what we hear in our own heads? Why is this?

Well, it's because inside our head we hear our voice in two different ways. The first is through vibrating sound waves hitting the ear drum and the second is through vibrating sound waves hitting the vocal cords – the combination of these gives us the idea that we have far more bass in our voices than we actually do. We then hear our voices as other people do and wonder why we sound so high-pitched, suddenly going from James Earl Jones (the voice of Darth Vader) to a 10-year-old girl.

Regardless of your current sound, you can practise and hone your voice to help you feel amazing when speaking.

Here are some vocal tips that work well:

- Remember that your voice is an instrument and warming it up is important. Try humming, tongue trills (if you can) or some tongue twisters, such as 'Suzy sitting in a shoe shine shop, all day long she sits and shines, all day long she shines and sits' (pro tip: say this fast for much hilarity!).
- When delivering a long talk, try speeding up your speech at times to create momentum, excitement or urgency, then slow it

right down in parts to create impact, intensity or sadness. One long speech delivered at the same pace could result in people switching off.

- You can also play with volume: be booming at some moments and then whisper at others. Whispering consciously can bring in your audience both literally, as they lean forwards to catch what you're saying, and figuratively.

Here are some vocal habits that don't work quite as well:

- SHOUTING constantly.
- Using a very timid, quiet voice. We want to hear your opinion, your point of view, your jokes, your excitement – we want to hear it all, because you're lovely!
- Be mindful of filler words (such as 'um' and 'err') or repetitive words (such as 'like' and 'literally'), which often come out when we're nervous. Notice what yours are and see if slowing down and pausing at points can help you to cut them out. We all have these, though, so don't be hard on yourself.

Remind yourself that you don't have to say everything perfectly and that we like and connect with people more when there's a humanness in how they talk. Perfection isn't connection. Remember that the more you do, the more you teach your brain you can.

How to public speak without the 'eek!'

The final piece of advice I suggest implementing is going to feel less comfortable, but it is truly the only way to grow in public speaking confidence, and it is this: start doing some public speaking. Start small. Challenge yourself to take baby steps and set yourself mini challenges. This might look like being the friend who gives everyone's order to the waiter, it might be volunteering to do a presentation or deliver training at work, or it might simply be finding opportunities to speak more in everyday conversations. Begin from where you are and know that you've got this. Here are some more action points to help get you started.

Inside:

1 **Prepare some positive self-talk.** Flick back to p. 21 and think of five positive phrases you could say to yourself before you next speak in public. These could be anything from 'You've got this, you're prepared and ready' to 'I'm so excited to share my new ideas with people.' Jot these down and keep them safe so they're easy to access next time you begin your presentation preparation. We've got to be on our own team, right?

2 **'Anchor' in a feeling of confidence** before a public speaking opportunity. Close your eyes and imagine a time when you felt your most confident self (this could be yesterday or it could be years ago). As you picture the moment, I want you to become aware of your body and any emotions you're feeling: excitement, pride and anything else that comes up for you. Feel what you feel, but also see what you see and hear what you hear. When your feelings of confidence are at their highest level, press your first finger and thumb together in a light pinch. Then open your eyes, stand up and shake it off, before going again, repeating the process three to five times. The pressing of the fingers eventually (with repetition) becomes an 'anchor' to the feeling of confidence, so you can use it for a confidence boost before a presentation. (I used this technique before I gave my TED Talk and, trust me, it works.)

3 **Change your focus.** When talking in front of other people we can often get fixated on the idea that people will be looking at us as we present and perhaps making a judgement on how well we do, which can feel like a lot of pressure. Therefore, switch your focus by reminding yourself that most people are far more concerned with the information you have to provide rather than how you as an individual actually present it. In a working environment, for example,

the information you have to share will probably be helping your audience to do their own jobs better, whether it's providing them with the latest research or sharing a new company process, so this is what their attention will be on, not you. Shifting the focus like this can help take the pressure off yourself to deliver a perfect performance.

Outside:

1 **Watch and learn.** Take some time to watch TED Talks or motivational speeches online. See if you can play 'great speaker bingo' by spotting the good movements, hand gestures and vocal techniques that we've discussed in this chapter. Have a go at copying any techniques you're drawn to – would you include any of them in your future public speaking? (I'm always keen to see great speakers, so if you spot anyone good then do send them my way via Instagram @iamhollymatthews)

2 **Talk nonsense.** This is a great technique for playing around with pitch, pace, pauses and projection without needing to get the words 'right'. For 30 seconds to one minute, talk utter nonsense. This means non-word gibberish or a made-up language that is not trying to mean anything. Deliver this nonsense as if giving the greatest speech of your life. By removing focus from the words, we allow ourselves more freedom to play around with everything else. Record yourself doing so. Even though this might feel very uncomfortable to watch back (at first), it's a great way to learn what's working in terms of your delivery and what could do with some tweaking.

3 **Play 'wing it'.** This is a useful game to practise your speaking skills and hone your ability to think on your feet, all from the comfort of your own home. Begin by writing down a list of 10 topics (or get a friend to), which could be anything from *Strictly Come Dancing* to the weather. Next, pick a topic from the list at random and talk about it for one minute. An alternative is to gather together a collection of objects or photographs and to take the same approach: pick up an

item at random and discuss it for one minute, either explaining what it is or making up a fun backstory (adding in as much detail and flavour as you can!). To take the game up a gear, film yourself doing this exercise so you can watch back your performance or imagine yourself speaking in different scenarios – some formal, some relaxed. This can help you lessen the anxiety that if you forgot your words, you'd have nothing to say.

Guest advice

Claira Hermet
BBC radio presenter and host
@missclairahermet

❝Here's the truth. A different version of us who has the tools to do whatever they want exists within all of us, so start from the end. Who is the version of us that can stand and talk confidently to a group of people? What do they think? How do they feel? How do they carry themselves? Then we do our best to embody those characteristics NOW. Will we get it right first time? Hell no. Will it be trial and error? Yes, babes!

My advice (and what I have practised in my own career) is telling myself: it's just fear… IT WON'T KILL YOU. If you aren't willing to go try … you've already failed, and so go try and prove to yourself YOU CAN.❞

#2

Social situations

At the age of 19, my sister Beki attended a house party with her friends. The event was in full swing, drinks were flowing, music was pumping and joy was being felt by many. In among this youthful party atmosphere, my sister confidently turned to the girl beside her and asked, 'Whose party is this, anyway?' to a girl who was, in fact, the host of the party.

It was just a silly, awkward, social faux pas that the party host has likely never given a second thought, but my sister keeps the shame she felt locked away in a bank of 'Beki's awkward social moments' that gets opened periodically with an anxiety-riddled shudder.

We're all Beki at times and, even as a social bunch of human beings, we can often find social interactions hard. I still regularly get overwhelmed at large events, where the chatter of lots of conversations can distract my mind, and without supporting myself (using the techniques we'll discuss in this chapter) I can leave feeling depleted.

In order for us to survive, though, we need other people. So, when we experience a kind of socially embarrassing moment, it can feel *way* bigger than the reality of it. This is because on a primal level the fear of being shunned from the group scares us. As we saw in the last chapter, in the days of our early ancestors we would group together for survival and although, thankfully, most of our worlds have shifted from the potential of being killed on a daily basis, this fear of being left out to fend for ourselves still sits under the surface.

Humans are a social species and we are built to rely on each other. When we are born, we need a parent or caregiver to help us stay alive. As we go through life, we need the help of other people – our friends, our co-workers, our family – to thrive, grow and assist us in bringing our ideas and dreams to life. I can have the best idea in the world but I'm always going to need other people to help it come to fruition.

Matthew Lieberman is a professor of psychology, psychiatry and bio-behaviour science at UCLA, and in his TED Talk he outlines how our 'social brain' and our ability to predict human behaviour is our superpower. Lieberman believes that human connection is as important to our health as not smoking and that being around people who love us can actually decrease our feelings of physical and mental pain. Lieberman even states that Maslow's hierarchy of needs (a pyramid-shaped model indicating our five innate needs as human beings) should be switched around to have 'love and belonging' as our most essential need at the base of the pyramid (as opposed to in its current position, where it's rated after our safety and physiological needs).

So, if science tells us that we need each other, why do so many of us find being in social situations challenging? In this chapter we're going to delve into why we sometimes feel awkward, how to build our social confidence and how to let go of worrying about what other people think. You see, I want you to win and create a life that feels great, but in order to have those things you are going to need to get social.

Will I be shy forever?

The discussion about nature versus nurture is an ongoing one and might seem a repetitive talking point at this stage, but we'll touch on it as we go because it's always interesting to see what genetic research has to tell us. Time and time again research has found that while we can safely say there are some genetic markers in all areas of our personality (i.e. the bits we're born with that we can't control), there are also parts of our personalities that we can shape, and this is where it gets interesting.

Just like other aspects of our genetics (such as eye colour, skin colour and the type of hair we have), we could dwell on the parts of our personalities that we can't change, and wish they were different, but the fact remains that there's no point in doing this. It is all part of the randomness of life and it's a fruitless exercise to focus on wishing it were different. So, under my watch, we don't waste time on that. Instead, we focus on what we can do and what we can change, and we get creative with the 'can'.

Interestingly enough, the trait of shyness is said to only be 30 per cent genetic with the rest based on external factors, such as how we grew up, the things we've seen in the world, and other circumstances and experiences beyond ourselves. Therefore, those of you who currently identify as shy, but wish to feel more confident, can rest assured that even with a genetic predisposition to shyness in place, there is still a lot you can do to support yourself in social situations.

I'm going to use myself as an anecdotal example of this. Meeting me now, people would assume that I have always found social interactions easy, but that couldn't be further from the truth. As a young child, I was excellent in situations where I knew the people I was talking to, but if I didn't, I would often feel trapped in my own mind. By this I mean I'd feel too scared to speak up but be having all these thoughts about what I would like to say. I was always way better at talking to adults than I was to my own peers, and as a neurodivergent person I often found myself studying other people like animals in a zoo, wondering what behaviour I should mimic so I could appear like everyone else.

Thankfully, though, this people studying served me well. I was taken to an acting class at a young age (most definitely prompted by the fact that I was considered shy in social settings), and I began to look

'**Confidence** allows us to walk into a room and feel **free. Free to be who you want to be** and **free to articulate yourself** (and your opinions) in whichever way you wish.'

at the outward appearance of the confident people in my class. I began to pretend to act like them, which allowed me to practise being a confident person, and over time this became my reality.

I get what it is like to feel shy, and I have experienced what it is like to feel confident. Confidence feels better. Confidence allows us to walk into a room and feel free. Free to be who you want to be and free to articulate yourself (and your opinions) in whichever way you wish. That is a true gift and that's why teaching confidence to others is so important to me.

Shyness versus introversion

Now let's also not get shyness confused with introversion. Based on psychologist Carl Yung's description of personality types, a person who is more introverted is someone who gets their energy by looking inwards, whereas somebody who is an extrovert gains their energy from outside sources. This doesn't mean that introverted people dislike time with others, it just means that they need time to reboot their energy on their own.

Moment to pause
Think about your own life for a second and consider if you feel more energised by going out for dinner with friends or by having a pamper night on your own. This doesn't mean you don't enjoy both, but perhaps you can see yourself leaning more towards one or other as a guaranteed way to reboot.

So, we can see that with this distinction, somebody could have the personality type of an extrovert but still be shy. In some respects, this must be one of the most challenging of mixes and it's certainly not something we hear about often. You have a person who is desperate to get their energy from social interaction but, due to a small genetic predisposition and a dollop of habit, feels shyness.

This might look like someone who takes a long time to open up to people, and as a result finds it hard to make friends, but on being left alone feels despondent. Once they have a friend or friends whom they trust, they then find themselves completely thriving on this human engagement.

I've always described myself as a confident introvert. I'm the opposite of the above. I really love people but can find myself being depleted after bouts of social interaction. To the outside world I've always looked like a traditional extrovert. I will chat your ear off, confidently work a room and have zero fear about who I am talking to (regardless of which room I'm in), but the minute I get home my social battery dies and I retreat into myself to re-energise.

Being shy and finding it hard socially is different to consciously knowing that you're an introvert and that you need time to build up your energy levels alone. Let's not confuse the two.

Moment to pause

I want you to feel empowered to make changes to support who you are, so it's important to reflect on yourself for a moment. How do you feel during and after social gatherings? How and when do you feel alive and energised? Where do you feel you sit on the introversion and extroversion scale? The answers to these questions don't matter to anyone else, but understanding your own personality type can help you to support yourself.

The extreme side of social shyness would be diagnosed as social anxiety, or social anxiety phobia, and this diagnostic disorder will likely require a deeper dive with talking therapies such as cognitive behavioural therapy (CBT), alongside the tips and tricks we will discuss here. As with all the work that I do, I believe in a multi-pronged attack at the challenges we face and I am a huge advocate of therapy (I have popped links to further resources on this on my website).

Let's get one important factor straight before we move into the meat of building our social confidence though: you are not alone if you find social stuff hard. It's reported that around 8 million people in the UK struggle with social anxiety disorder and it's the third most common mental condition in the world. That is *a lot* of people! So, wherever you sit in terms of personality type and the spectrum of shyness, I promise you that the behaviours you currently have in social settings can be adapted and changed, starting today.

Tricky social situations

It's now time to have a gander at which areas of being social we might find difficult. I asked The Happy Me Project community for their input on when they felt their least confident in social settings and this is what they came up with, in no particular order. Can I get a drum roll please…

- Meeting new people.
- Talking in big groups.
- Chatting on the phone.
- Asking and answering questions in front of others.
- The school run and small talk.
- Any kind of small talk (my daughter Texas calls this 'small chat', which makes me chuckle).
- Eating in front of others.
- Special occasions, such as weddings, where there is more expectation.
- Asking for help in a shop.
- Ordering food.
- Complaining about bad service.
- Networking events.

Of course, there will be so many other situations that are specific to you, so do feel free to message me on Instagram (@iamhollymatthews) so I can add your own flavour of socially uncomfortable situations to my ever-growing list.

Now let's get real: you will never completely escape moments of human awkwardness and that's OK. You are human. It's important, however, to start looking at your main triggers and finding ways to support yourself during these interactions that you struggle with.

You might be tricked into thinking, 'I've got to this age OK, why does it really matter if I'm awkward and don't do things because I feel unconfident socially?' Well, if you really feel 'it doesn't matter' then I guess it doesn't. You're the person who knows yourself the best and you have complete autonomy over your own life. But please be mindful that this feeling of 'why does it really matter?' could be your brain's way of copping out because it doesn't really want to do the hard work of stepping out of your comfort zone.

No judgement here – your brain is excellent and it is doing exactly what it is supposed to be doing. It has experienced something that made it feel unsafe in a social setting in the past and has decided it doesn't fancy feeling that way again. So, it offers up excuses to stop you putting yourself in situations that may be similar. That's how your brain is supposed to work, so it's doing its job.

Since you're here, though, I'm going to ask you to explore the possibility that your life might feel a whole lot better if some of your daily interactions flowed better and felt less uncomfortable.

In The Happy Me Project community, one of my lovely members shared that a social trigger for her is bumping into someone she knows from her school days or the past generally. She worries this person might judge her or, worse still, may not remember her at all, which would make her feel insignificant.

Another was worried by the thought of going to her husband's work event and being left with his colleagues' partners. She said that when this happens she always becomes very quiet and doesn't know what to say.

And two more members shared that their biggest fears were networking events at their companies where they are expected to mingle and get to know people. One of them said it makes them so nervous that they feel like calling in sick and never going to work again.

Many members said that since the pandemic they've found small talk generally to be stressful. This is understandable because we were locked away from other people for so long, and working from home is now a norm, so many of us are simply still out of practice when it comes to daily socialising.

You might see yourself in some of these experiences. Or perhaps you're like another client of mine who worked with me on getting comfortable going to mum and baby groups. She used the tools in this chapter and went from feeling anxious and stressed to being the person who organises the after-session meet-ups at a local cafe.

Consider your own world and which social situations bring you out in a cold sweat. Perhaps think about the last week or two and the things you've done. Is there anything that has felt challenging or that you wish could have been different? Consider the various areas of your life, such as work, friendships, family and anything social linked to these. When you have pinpointed your social triggers, I suggest you jot them down somewhere. Then, as we make our way through the chapter, you can note next to each trigger the different ideas and techniques you'd like to try to support yourself in each situation.

A note on the internet

Before we move on, I'd like to acknowledge how the rise of social media has had a big impact on how we're, well, social. Everything is posted online these days, so comparison, and the fear and anxiety that come with this, is rife. It wouldn't be surprising, then, if some of our concerns come from worrying that we won't be able to keep up with what we see online.

Interestingly, studies have also explored whether our overuse of online interaction is impairing our ability to connect in real life – for example, whether socially awkward people spend more time online *because* they are already socially awkward, and thus online activity feels like a nice alternative to in-person interactions. Or whether people who over-rely on virtual socialising *become* socially awkward because they have missed out on the chance to learn social skills and social confidence in person.

It's tricky to get a definitive answer but a recent study by Cecilia Brown, who works in the psychology department at Connecticut College, has indicated that more time online equals a worsening ability to deal with face-to-face interactions. This seems to make sense to me because practice makes perfect, so the fewer opportunities we have to practise our social skills in person (including all the body language that goes with that) then the less confident we'll be with it.

How to change your beliefs about socialising (aka your 'social stories')

In this section we will be talking about what I call our 'stories'. Essentially, these are created when we have a belief about something and it becomes so ingrained that it becomes a story we've created for ourselves in our minds.

Our brains like things to be packaged neatly into a narrative, you see. So, whenever we get new information, the brain is looking for patterns and similar experiences we've had in the past that may relate to this new one. If the brain is unsure about a new experience, it may fill in the gaps with, essentially, complete guesswork based on these past beliefs and experiences. Therefore you will see that a story can be helpful or unhelpful.

Here, we will focus on uncovering the negative stories we have created for ourselves about socialising (and the beliefs that helped create them) so that we can learn to replace them with better ones to support us.

The negative stories we create

I used to have the story that I wasn't good at networking. The story I told myself came from these beliefs: I'm not good at networking because I can't remember people's names, I will talk too much and networking events are all a bit too serious for me.

I based my beliefs on having been to a maximum of two work networking events where I felt uncomfortable, found the events themselves rather uninspiring and forgot someone's name once. It only took two uncomfortable occasions (and one forgotten name) for me to create a whole negative narrative around networking as a whole, and lots of beliefs to fuel this story.

I find it fascinating how quickly our brains can change from positive or neutral feelings about a situation to negative ones (and the colourful stories and beliefs we create to back up how we feel). One difficult conversation with someone at your friend's birthday gathering (where you lost your train of thought midway through and had to admit 'I don't know where I was going with that…') and your brain might conclude: 'I'm terrible at meeting new people' or 'I don't like parties.'

Once the brain has shifted to this negative space about a situation it is incredible just how convincing our internal excuses, or limiting beliefs, become. This happens because the brain is trying to protect us from ever having to feel like that again.

The stories we tell ourselves about anything in our lives will always be the reality that we see in front of us. So, we have to get really mindful and tread very carefully when we develop these stories. It's important to periodically check in to see if our stories are still serving us.

Identifying and dismantling your negative stories

Let's work through this section step by step to identify and dismantle our negative stories. You might find it helpful to grab a notebook and pen so you can make notes as we go.

Step 1: Consider the social triggers that you identified earlier (*see* p. 45). If you wrote these down, let's get them back out now.

Step 2: Write down the beliefs you currently hold about each of these social triggers. To identify your beliefs, write down in sentence form what you'd normally say about each social situation and how it makes you feel. For example, if 'eating in front of others' is your social trigger then you might have beliefs such as 'I'm always really awkward when I eat and I know people can tell' or 'I have bad table manners and it makes me embarrassed.'

Step 3: Take a step back and identify the overall story that these beliefs have shaped.

To give you some inspiration, I'm sharing three examples from when I recently did this exercise with one of my clients.

Example 1

Social trigger: Small talk with my neighbours
Beliefs about this trigger: 'I just don't have anything to say and I will embarrass myself'; 'My old neighbour always seemed annoyed at me and I think it's because he heard me and my partner arguing'; 'I saw my neighbour talking to another neighbour so it must be that he doesn't like me and he's ignoring me'; 'My neighbours' gardens are so nice and mine is overgrown, I bet they think I'm a mess.'
Social story: 'I never get on with my neighbours.'

Example 2

Social trigger: Work parties
Beliefs about this trigger: 'I make a fool of myself at parties'; 'Everyone always looks better than me and I know they'll be cringing at my outfit'; 'My colleagues think I'm weird and my boss doesn't like me'; 'Everyone judges me for not wanting to drink.'
Social story: 'Work parties are awful and I'm awkward at them.'

Example 3

Social trigger: Meeting my partner's family
Beliefs about this trigger: 'My ex-partner's family were standoffish with me and I don't think they liked me'; 'I bet they think I'm not good enough for my partner'; 'My partner's family are so smart that I never know what to say.'
Social story: 'I'm not good with the family of my partner.'

Step four: Now that you've identified your social stories, we're going to start calling them out because – and this is important to remember – these stories are *not* facts. They are merely your brain's interpretation of an experience that you've had in the past and, since they are not facts, this means you can decide to change them.

So, let's challenge these stories by looking again at the beliefs that created them. Take each belief in turn. Imagine yourself as the prosecutor in a court room. The belief is on the stand and you're cross-examining it. For each belief, go through each of the three questions below and answer honestly:

1. What is the **fear** that my belief is rooted in?

2. What is the **evidence** to support this belief? And the evidence to **dispute** it?

3. If I choose to keep this belief, what will be the **long-term impact**?

To get you started, here's an example from my client Claire as we completed this exercise together:

Social trigger: The staffroom at work
Beliefs about this trigger: 'No one speaks to me because they don't like me'; 'Everyone else makes friends easily'; 'I'm weird and no one is going to want to sit with me.'
Social story: 'I will never have friends at work.'

We began with Claire's belief that 'I'm weird and no one is going to want to sit with me.' I asked Claire about the **fear** that this belief was rooted in and she said, 'that I'll always be the one sat on my own every day, so I'll be lonely, and it's embarrassing because I'm just not very likeable.'

We then spent time looking at the **evidence** that Claire had gathered to support this fear. She shared that at a past workplace there had been an occasion when her colleagues had sat on one table and shared a pack of biscuits while laughing and joking together. There wasn't room for Claire to sit down and no one noticed or invited her in, so she was left sitting alone.

Claire said that lots of people have friends at work but she's never spent time with her colleagues outside of work, so she's concluded that there must be something wrong with her and that no one at work likes her. This had helped cement Claire's social story that she will never have friends at work.

I then asked Claire to **dispute** the evidence of her belief, to which she admitted that she often chose to sit alone at lunch. She also often went out for lunch, so probably hadn't given her colleagues a chance to get to know her. Her colleague Gemma had copied her into an email about a baby shower but Claire had ignored it as she thought maybe it was a mistake.

Lastly, I asked Claire what the **long-term impact** might be if she holds on to this belief. She recognised that if she continued to distance herself then she would create the scenario she feared most, since she would not be giving people the chance to become her friend.

Now I am not deluded enough to think that we will be able to get rid of the unhelpful stories we hold and the beliefs that fuel them overnight, but deciding that we want to break free from them, and completing the exercise above, is an important first step.

Creating new positive stories for yourself

The next phase is to begin replacing our unhelpful stories with more positive ones. How we talk to ourselves about our ability to be social is key to our success. Words matter – every word that we use indicates to our brains how we would like to see the world.

When thinking of positive stories to help us feel confident socially, we might have just one that feels powerful enough as a standalone story, or you may choose to have a whole array to fall back on. You also might decide that you would like some general statements to apply to all social situations, such as: 'I get more confident being social each day'; 'I am constantly learning and I embrace new experiences'; and 'I trust my instincts and it's OK to make mistakes.' Or perhaps you'd prefer to take each of your specific social triggers in turn and choose positive stories that directly correspond to each one.

For example, my client who believed she would never make friends at work came up with three positive stories to help with that specific situation:

- 'I am open to getting to know those around me.'
- 'I have friends outside of work and I can make friends at work.'
- 'When I am interested in my colleagues, they become interested in me too.'

Take a moment now and write out either 10 general positive stories or three positive stories for each of your social triggers.

When you have these jotted down, it's now on to the fun part of embedding these positive beliefs into your life. My favourite way of doing this is to post these statements around my home. Perhaps pop them on a sticky note in a high-traffic area (by the front door or on a mirror) or, if you're a whiteboard fan like me (I currently have about eight or nine!), then you can use these.

It's important to attach these new stories to things that happen in your daily life, too. For example, if you have a social event in your calendar coming up, I suggest that you look at your list of empowering beliefs, pick one, and then say it to yourself every time you think about or prepare for this event – for example, 'I am great at socialising.' Connecting your empowering belief with a time when you're being social will help your brain to link you being social with a positive experience. This in time will help chip away at your old BS stories that were holding you back.

Why practice makes perfect

I appreciate that initially saying these positive statements to yourself is going to be a little uncomfortable, and your brain might even try to rebel against your efforts, but stick with it. The repetition of this work is key. You see, prior to doing this work your brain created a neural pathway based on an experience and the unhelpful stories you have told it. I like to imagine this brain pathway as a huge green grassy field (bear with me).

In this field is a heavily trodden-down path of grass. This is where you have walked many times before and you have flattened down the grass with the repetition of walking that same path. This path is easy, it's familiar and it is the path of least resistance. If we relate this back to the beliefs we have about a social situation, this path is your unhelpful stories pathway, such as 'I just stay quiet in social situations because it's easier' or 'I won't speak to those new people, because what if I mess up?'

Now that you're here and have decided to build your confidence in social settings, you are creating a new pathway. The first few times you cross that field of thick grass will be hard. You will come up against some resistance and it will take much repetition before the new path becomes the easier one of the two to walk along.

There will even be some days when you will sneak down that old flattened, easier pathway (because it's familiar and habitual). Over time, though, with practice and repetition, the new, more positive pathway will become *the* pathway and the old route of avoidance in social situations will become overgrown and less hospitable. I know you're ready to pop on your walking boots and stomp along your new path, so let's go. You've got this!

How to hold a conversation

We have looked at how we talk to ourselves, so now let's think about how we talk to others.

Not everybody goes into social settings as a natural conversationalist. And, aside from being taught the basics of speech as a child, no one ever really teaches you how to hold a conversation if it doesn't come naturally to you.

As an actress, I like a script, and in social settings it is totally acceptable to have considered your own social script too, such as the conversations you're likely to have at any given event. It is also perfectly appropriate to rehearse and practise these conversations beforehand if you're feeling anxious.

So, for those of us who find this stuff hard, let me offer some conversational guidance for creating your own social script. This comes in the form of a simple three-step conversational template that can be broken into **A.R.E.**:

1. **A**nchor

2. **R**eveal

3. **E**ncourage

Let's look at each of these steps in turn.

Step 1: notice an Anchor. The anchor is a shared reality between you and the other people in the social situation. This could be the venue, time of year, weather or reason for the social gathering. For this example, let's say you're at a friend's wedding.

Step 2: Reveal. The reveal is when you say something about the anchor. For example, 'What a gorgeous wedding venue this is' or 'I can't believe how lucky they have been with the weather today.'

Step 3: Encourage. By this we mean asking a question based on the anchor or reveal to encourage the conversation along, such as 'How do you know the couple?' or 'Did you travel far to be here?'

Having this A.R.E. template to hand is a useful starter kit if you're feeling nervous about everyday conversations, or for times when you feel you need some support. Over time, you'll work out some generic anchor ideas, reveal statements and encourage questions, which will give you a bank of ideas that you can fall back on in any situation. Below are some more ideas to help get you started.

1. Anchor ideas:

* Talk about something you can hear, e.g. music or a speech.
* Talk about something you can taste, e.g. the lovely wedding cake.
* Talk about something you can see, e.g. the bride's dress or Uncle John going wild on the dance floor.
* Talk about the weather (a staple of British small talk).
* Talk about a recent event, e.g. a big football tournament.
* Talk about something based on the time of year, e.g. Christmas, New Year, a change of season, back-to-school time.
* Talk about something based on an aspect of the person, e.g. they are walking a dog, pushing a baby in a pushchair or wearing a fabulous outfit.

2. Reveal ideas:

* 'What a great speech!'; 'What a beautiful choice of music.'
* 'Wow this cake is delicious!'; 'Oh, I really need this cup of tea.' (I'm popping this in because I say this at least twice a day...)
* 'The bride looks incredible; I love the sleeves on that dress'; 'I see Uncle John is busting out his signature moves again.'
* 'How typically British that it would start to rain as soon as we went outside!'; 'I can't believe how hot it's been over the last few months.'

- 'I'm hoping we will get back to catch the end of the match'; 'What a perfect way to end the week, first a big football win and now this.'
- 'I'm so looking forward to Christmas this year, now my kids are old enough to appreciate it'; 'Not long till the kids are back at school!'
- 'Oh gosh your dog is adorable'; 'What a lovely coat that is, so vibrant!'

3. Encourage ideas:

- 'What type of music are you into?'; 'Do you know the best man?'
- 'Did you enjoy the starter? I nearly chose the same one'; 'Are you a tea or coffee person?'
- 'Did you have a traditional wedding?'; 'Have you witnessed Uncle John doing "the worm" before?'
- 'Are you going on holiday this year?'; 'How has work been for you in this heat?'
- 'Do you like football?'; 'Who do you support?'; 'Do you get to the games much?'
- 'Are you doing anything nice for Christmas?'; 'How have the summer holidays been with four kids?'; 'Are you looking forward to getting back to work in September?'

A reminder: a conversation is a tennis match, a back-and-forth where everyone has a chance to speak. The pressure isn't on you to fill every gap. This can be comforting to remember as you aren't on show; the other person has their part to play, too. But having a few go-to questions in your back pocket can be your fall-back serve of the conversational ball. So, next time you feel anxious about an event, I challenge you to come up with a list of conversation starters and topics before you arrive. Good luck, it's going to be fun!

Worrying about what others think

As I write this, I am sitting in a cafe in a suburb of Newcastle upon Tyne. It's a very cool, hipster sort of place, filled with middle-class yummy mummies and university students. I've never been here before and, as I walked in, heads turned to look my way. I took a seat at a table alone and pulled out my laptop to begin writing.

I have zero doubt that as those heads turned to take in the new addition to the space, each person reflected on who I am. They will have considered how I carry myself, my body language, my dress sense and myriad other things. In fact, a study at Princeton University showed that it takes just one tenth of a second to come to some pretty big judgements about others, including attractiveness, trustworthiness, likeability, competence and aggressiveness.

With the knowledge of this research, we could choose to be concerned about this and tie ourselves in knots, or we could recognise a few other truths too. Sure, there will be judgement, that's human nature and a protection mechanism we all have, but everyone is only ever looking at you through one lens. They're looking through their own model of the world, based on their own experiences, and this means that every single person will come to a different conclusion, and none of them is definitively right.

The other (and in my opinion) more important truth is this: people are far more worried about what they are doing than what you are doing. Although those cafe-goers glanced my way and made their human judgements, they also very quickly continued with their caramel lattes. Many of them will have spent way longer considering how I was perceiving them than thinking about me.

I am going to hazard a guess and say that when most of us walk into a room, we have an awareness of how *we* look, *our* hair, *our* make-up, *our* outfit or what *we* are doing, and very little time is spent chewing over whether the woman in the corner of the room needs to get her roots done or whether that young mum sounds interesting as she chats to her friend.

No one really cares what you're doing. That might even be a little disappointing in some respects, but in terms of building social confidence, it's great to remember.

As a ridiculous study of this (and because I am rarely plagued by social embarrassment now, having done the silliest things as an actor), I once tried to prove to a friend that people don't really care what anyone else is doing by barking like a dog on Oxford Street in London. For those unaware of this street, it's one of the busiest spots in the city and is full to the brim with every type of person you can imagine. Guess what happened as I gave my best hound-dog impression? Nothing. People barely looked up and those who did quickly moved on. The friend I was with, of course, was mortified, but I proved my point (loudly).

Grounding techniques for entering a new space

So now we know that no one is really paying that much attention, let's throw in some lovely grounding techniques to help us feel as good as possible when walking into a new space.

To ground ourselves, essentially, means to stay connected to the present moment and to not get lost in our thoughts. When we feel anxious, we can very quickly get into our heads, by which I mean we begin considering every possible negative outcome and worrying about all of them. This can make us feel quite out of alignment with our surroundings and even result in us feeling disconnected from our bodies.

Use of our senses

When entering a new space, it's helpful to focus your attention on your senses to help you feel present. Notice what you can **see**, **hear** and **feel** as you step in. Bring your awareness to your feet, planting them firmly on the floor. Then notice your steps, the carpet, the wooden floor or the concrete. Change your focus to the specific things you can see in a room as you walk in and simply acknowledge their existence. Then turn your attention to what you can hear.

I see a woman writing on her laptop, a picture of a flower on the wall and a gorgeous cake display.

I hear chatting, a radio show and the sound of a coffee machine being used.

I feel the hard wooden floor beneath my feet, the warmth of my coat and the leather strap of my bag.

Having an awareness of the room will help keep you in the room and out of your head.

Use of props

Some of my clients like to use a prop to help them feel grounded, too – an anchor for feeling calm. They might pop a crystal stone or something small such as a marble in their pocket, and subtly hold on to these items when they enter a new space. Personally, I love a crystal in my pocket. I don't think they have special powers, but I like the look of them, I like the feel of them and they're easy to carry as a reminder that I choose to be calm.

We can use a prop in this way because we draw the anxious energy we might feel into focusing on the object we can feel in our pocket instead. I have even had a client who would pop a coin in her shoe to

'When entering a new space, it's helpful to **focus your attention on your senses** to help you feel present. Notice what you can <u>**see**</u>, <u>**hear**</u> and <u>**feel**</u> as you step in.'

draw her attention into the moment. She could feel the coin (it didn't cause discomfort) and this brought her out of her worry thoughts and into the present situation.

These little tools may seem simple and silly, but honestly, it's often the stuff we think can't possibly work that does. So don't be afraid to experiment with different ideas to find out what works best for you. Please most definitely send me your own weird and wonderful coping strategies when you find them by messaging me on Instagram (@iamhollymatthews) so I can give them a go myself too!

Being a human being is embarrassing – how to deal with it

Imagine this. You're a brand-new mum, your baby is barely a week old. You're tired, full of hormones and have spent the last hour tidying your home in preparation for a health visitor. Anyone who has ever had this type of visit to their home will know that it can be a little nerve-wracking, even when you know everything is in order.

The doorbell rings, you take one last look around and open the door with a bright smile on your face. You invite the person at your door into your home and ask them to take off their shoes. You then usher a rather perplexed-looking person towards a Moses basket and your tiny sleeping baby as she stares blankly and says nothing.

By now you're beginning to believe that this person is rather rude and not in the slightest bit interested in doing their job. But then they open their mouth and say, 'I've come to pick up the ironing.' It's at this point that you remember you booked somebody to take care of your clothes this week, and that this is in fact *not* your health visitor (and if you'd not been so tired, you'd have realised a health visitor would have definitely shown some ID!).

You see, being a human is awkward. It's littered with cringe-filled moments, mistakes and failings and it can all feel a bit chaotic. You aren't alone in this.

There isn't a person out there who hasn't experienced an excruciatingly embarrassing moment in their lives. I asked The Happy Me Project community what some of their awkward social moments were, and here is a selection of some of my faves:

- Ending a work call by saying 'love you'.
- Returning a wave only to realise that someone wasn't really waving at you.
- Losing your balance on a train and falling into someone's lap.
- When you tell a story in a group, realise no one is listening and then very slowly get quieter, hoping that no one noticed.
- Having had lots of interactions with someone, forgetting their name but knowing it's gone too far to ask, so just silently committing to having to call them a generic 'mate' or 'love' until the end of time.
- Not hearing someone the first time they say something, asking them to repeat what they said, and then still not understanding, so you just nod, mumble something and hope you haven't offended them.

Did your toes curl just reading some of these? I bet you can relate to a few and possibly even got whisked back to your own mortifying moment (sorry about that).

We can't die of embarrassment, though. Although sometimes it does feel like we're coming horribly close, as our faces flush red and our hearts pump hard in our chests. But despite how it might feel, death isn't nearby, so we simply have to ride out these moments – and possibly even have a hilarious story to tell people in the future.

The challenge we face with embarrassing moments, though, is that we may then be tempted to try to avoid ever being in a similar social situation again. This could lead to us turning the situation into one of the social triggers that we spoke about earlier (see p. 43). It also means, if we avoid the same scenario again, that we're holding on to the embarrassment for longer, while also robbing ourselves of the opportunity to learn to bounce back from these inevitable social mishaps. This is because the more we expose ourselves to situations where we might make social blunders, the more we grow resilient to them, and the better we become at dealing with any social mishaps moving forward.

I wish the route to building our social confidence was an easier one. A journey where we didn't have to feel uncomfortable or make mistakes. A journey where we didn't have to grow from saying things like, 'I saw you brought your mum, that's sweet' to a man who was at a birthday party with his new girlfriend who happened to be a bit older than him (a brave story shared by someone who follows me on Instagram). But the tough stuff is all part of the process.

We can't protect ourselves from the inevitable social mishaps and embarrassment that come with being human, but that doesn't mean we have to dive in at the deep end and force ourselves to be in the busiest social settings or the most triggering situations from day one. We can absolutely ease ourselves into the social pool, so to end this chapter let me share with you my favourite technique for building confidence socially. Think of my Four Ps technique as social armbands, if you will.

The Four Ps system

This is a tried-and-tested system that I use with clients (and myself) as a support guide in social situations. It's a template that you can use when tackling one of your triggering social situations (after having done lots of the lovely unpicking of the stories work covered earlier in the chapter):

1. Prepare

2. Practise

3. People

4. Pause

Let's look at each step in turn.

1. Prepare

Set an intention for your interactions beforehand. This might be 'I want to speak to at least one new person at the party' or 'I want to spend at least one hour mingling at the networking event.' This is your choice and a nice way to challenge yourself ahead of time.

Preparing might also include the logistics of where you're going. Parking, what to wear, who will be there and what you will need to bring with you. Preparing things ahead of time is going to help you feel more in control. This will make some elements feel more predictable and will allow you to cope better when it sometimes gets unpredictable.

Prepare may also mean bringing things that can help to support you being social (inner-ear headphones or anxiety jewellery, for example). It could also mean letting someone else know ahead of time how you're feeling and preparing *them* for any support they can give you. As an example, I always ask my children to deliberately interrupt and ask someone's name when they're with me as they know I have some anxiety around not remembering names. A client of mine has a code word with her husband for when she is feeling overwhelmed, and he then knows to make an excuse to take her outside for some fresh air. Let people help you.

2. Practise

Practise speaking out loud and introducing yourself. Practise fake conversations. Even though we cannot ever know for sure what other people will say, we can often make a good guess at some things that will come up! Skip back to the ideas on p. 54 to remind yourself of some conversation ideas and questions to practise.

You could also practise the journey to and from a venue or try on your outfit or hairstyle. My husband Ross used to do his hair and beard a week or two before a wedding or big event to see roughly how long it would take to grow to a length he liked. He used to call it doing a 'mock head', which always made me laugh.

3. People

This is the bit where you are around people, the social bit. As you do this, you can support yourself with the grounding techniques discussed earlier (see p. 58). Perhaps some calm breathing might help too, so you could experiment with the techniques from pp. 24 and 67. You could also support yourself by periodically checking for tension in your body (releasing tension from your forehead, shoulders and jaw that you may not even be aware you're holding). This doesn't have to be anything anyone else is aware of, but if you know you're a jaw clencher and you're feeling some anxiety, take a nice full breath in through your nose and on the outbreath focus your attention on your jaw and release the tightness you're experiencing.

Don't be afraid to step out of the situation to take breaks and remember to let go of the notion that everything has to be perfect. You're here, so smile, find the fun and remember that lots of people in the room are probably feeling a little nervous, too.

4. Pause

This is your time after being social. A time to decompress, breathe a sigh of relief and give a little whoop of well done. A time to process what you did well, what needs a bit more practice, and to discover if there are areas you need to change a little for next time. This is a chance to recognise the pressure you may have put on yourself before being social and to acknowledge how most of the things you worried about likely didn't happen.

As an overthinking human, I know that this is the time when rumination and regret may sneak in, and if you're not careful you might play out the social event over and over in your mind. Your mantra to kill this behaviour is as follows: 'Huh, that's interesting.' For example, 'Huh, that's interesting that I was comfortable talking to Jade but when her cousin arrived, I felt awkward' or 'Huh, that's interesting that when I arrived at the party, I felt like the woman in the red dress didn't like me yet we had a lovely conversation later in the night.'

Take time to reflect and gently analyse how things went without judgement of yourself, just noticing and allowing your reflection to guide your next bout of social interaction. It's your nudge to recognise the lessons from the day and which areas you can practise more for next time.

Make sure to check for your own biases about how the event played out and where you might be making assumptions about someone else's behaviour. It's always worth tuning in to which version of yourself you might have been bringing to the table, and how this might impact the lens you're seeing things through. Was she really looking at you 'funny' or was

'Remember that you are a **work in progress** and every time you step out into the world and try something new, you are teaching your brain **that you can.**'

she admiring your outfit? When we might be feeling less than our best, our brains may interpret the situation with a negative bias.

And lastly, be proud of yourself for taking on this challenge! You're doing so great. Take some time to do something lovely for yourself and reward your effort. Remember that you are a work in progress and every time you step out into the world and try something new, you are teaching your brain that you can.

From no-showing to outgoing

To help you put into practice the techniques we've discussed in this chapter, here are some action points to get you started.

Inside:

1 **Visualisation.** Practise social situations in your mind before taking steps in real life. Pick situations you would like to be in and imagine yourself in them, dealing with the conversations and atmosphere with ease. See yourself confidently navigating it all, with your shoulders back, head held high and a smile on your face. Make this visualisation part of your daily routine – I'm a before-bed sort of visualiser, and I do it every night.

2 **Learn to breathe.** Breathwork is a powerful tool in grounding yourself and calming anxiety. This can be used before being social and even during it. Here are a few styles you can try:

- Humming breath is where you breathe in through your nose for five seconds and on the outbreath you hum for five seconds (the vibration of the humming can help calm your nervous system).
- Pursed lips breathing requires you to breathe in through your nose for four, and on the outbreath breathe slowly through your mouth with pursed lips (as if blowing out a candle) for four.

More breathing techniques can be found on p. 24.

3 **Set a challenge.** Write a list of social challenges made up of things that you currently find hard to do. This could be asking for help while in a supermarket, asking a stranger for directions or having a conversation with someone in the gym. Write out 20 tasks to start with and decide how many you will do per week. Each time you do one, tick it off and pat yourself on the back. The more you do, the easier it will become (you just have to get through the tough beginning bit, which I know you can do!). Make sure to share your wins with me on Instagram (@iamhollymatthews), so I can celebrate with you.

Outside:

1 **Try mirroring.** This is the art of mimicking someone's confident body language, vocal style, pace, tone or even attitude (we do this subconsciously when we like someone). We can use this to our advantage when we want to connect by subtly mirroring what someone is doing. This might be by sitting in a similar position to the person, leaning forwards or backwards as they are, or picking up the pace or tone of their speech. Be mindful to only imitate positive behaviour and do it very subtly.

2 **Watch your feet.** When we are anxious our body gets ready for fight or flight and may convey indicators that we need to get away. When you are enjoying a conversation with someone your feet will naturally point towards them, but when you're nervous you might find you have shifted your feet to point away (or perhaps your whole body is angled in a different direction). If you want to appear confident and engaged, then stop your feet trying to retreat by angling them towards the person you're talking to.

3 **Open and unblock.** Blocking is body language that creates a barrier between us and the 'danger', which in this instance is people. Blocking body language might look like crossing your arms, touching your eyes or mouth, or holding something like a bag in front of you. When in social situations and meeting new people, try to focus on open and warm postures, open palms and hand gestures, and smiling. Nodding now and then in agreement with the other person as they speak can also work well in creating open body language.

Guest advice

Helen Thorn
Comedian and best-selling author
@itsmehelenthorn one half of @scummymummies

❝Social settings and anxiety go hand in hand. It is so normal to feel overwhelmed in social settings, and to assume that at any given moment you're going to make a colossal dickhead of yourself.

My little tip is, before you go out, make a quick list of three qualities you like about yourself and why your loved ones think you're wonderful. This is like a little hug to yourself and a confidence boost. Remember that everyone else is too busy worrying if they're going embarrass themselves and authenticity is the best way to connect with the good people in this life. Also, there is nothing wrong with leaving an event early if you're not feeling it!❞

#3

Standing up for yourself

I am a nice human. I'm kind, thoughtful and, like every human on this planet (even those who pretend otherwise), I want to be liked.

When I was younger, that desire to be the 'nice girl', who was liked, sometimes meant that I wasn't always assertive and I would put my own needs way down on the list of priorities. It also meant that, on occasion, I slipped very heavily into people pleasing (which we shall talk about soon), and I was pushed around by more domineering characters. As I got older, I learned a few tools to help me become more confident in standing up for myself and my needs, and that's what I'm going to share with you here.

Now, depending on where you currently are with your communication style, I know that standing up for yourself and being assertive might feel a little intimidating. If that's you, then that's OK. As with the rest of this book, you won't be alone and you can take things at a pace that feels comfortable for you. I'm going to coach you through each stage of this journey and the first step is to understand the different communication styles available to us. Let's begin.

What does 'being assertive' mean?

Assertiveness, in a nutshell, is the holy grail mix of standing up for your own rights and needs, while also respecting the rights and needs of others.

When people think of being assertive, it can sometimes get conflated with aggressiveness or being domineering. Perhaps when you think of someone being assertive you imagine a Max Belfort character from *The Wolf of Wall Street*, bullishly barking orders at his friends and co-workers. But, actually, this is not assertiveness.

There are generally considered to be four main communication styles: passive, passive-aggressive, aggressive and assertive. The first three are problematic, while the fourth, assertiveness (and the focus of this chapter), is a confident and direct style of communication that we should all ideally be aiming for.

Let's start then by taking a scenario to show how the first three styles of communication might play out. As you read through each style below, consider where an assertive style may work better. Perhaps also note if any of these three styles feels more natural to you.

Scenario

Kevin from work keeps eating the custard cream biscuits that you brought in from home. Today, when you went to have a biscuit with your cup of tea, there were none left.

Behaviour 1: passive
You don't say anything to Kevin. It's nice to share and you wouldn't want Kevin to feel bad or to think less of you by not sharing your food. You choose to stay quiet although, if you're honest, you're disappointed to miss out on the sweet treat.

Behaviour 2: passive-aggressive

You don't say anything directly to Kevin, but you do make snarky comments, while he's in earshot, about how you never have any biscuits to dunk in your tea. Plus, you most definitely moan about him in the break room to anyone who will listen.

Behaviour 3: aggressive

Upon finding the biscuits have been eaten, you scream at Kevin like a demented banshee and tell him just how selfish and greedy he is being (with veins sticking out of your bright red face as you do so). You *demand* back the biscuits you brought in.

As you can hopefully see, none of these three styles of communication is conducive to a happy life for anyone. The passive version means you're not getting your needs met because you're frustrated and 'biscuit-less'. The passive-aggressive version means your needs are still not met, plus you're leaking out irritation through your coded comments and making everyone around biscuit-gate feel uncomfortable. Lastly, the aggressive stance means you do get your needs met but at what cost? You metaphorically torch everything else around you, as you deny your colleagues their right for a calm and respectful workplace. Plus you possibly get in trouble with your boss.

Now, let's look at the coveted fourth style in the same scenario:

Behaviour 4: assertive

You approach Kevin with the following: 'Hi Kevin, I've noticed that you're eating the custard creams from the break room. I'm not sure that you're aware but those are my custard creams. Now while I am more than happy to share, I felt disappointed today that there were none of my biscuits left to dip in my cup of tea. As you are also a lover of the custard cream, perhaps we could come up with a schedule that means I buy some one week and then you buy some the next, making the situation fair for all.'

This approach lets Kevin know how you feel and what you want, without attacking him personally (for all we know, he may be unaware that these are your biscuits). It is of course a very light-hearted example, but I hope it highlights the very different communication styles available to us.

As part of The Happy Me Project membership, I ran a session in which we discussed everyone's personal communication styles. We found that quite a few people identified as mostly passive but said that at breaking point (or if triggered by certain people) they'd fly from passive straight to aggressive, i.e. say nothing then scream everything. This means not speaking our truth until we can't restrain it any longer, when it comes out in an unmanaged way. We found that not many of us used an assertive style regularly, and I think that makes sense because assertiveness isn't often modelled around us. It's also not really something we're ever taught, so lots of us simply don't know where to begin.

Worry not though, my lovely friend, because you're in the right place to learn to be assertive now. I want you to see that you can still be kind and get what you want. You do not need to bulldoze or dominate everyone else to assert your needs, and you don't have to change your whole personality to bring in being assertive.

Why don't we act assertive?

When my daughter Brooke started school, she became fast friends with a girl called Emily. Emily was a hugger and every morning she would squeeze Brooke tightly with a big happy grin on her face. The little girl was a lot bigger than Brooke and the hugs smothered her tiny frame, which Brooke began to dread. Emily was a lovely girl whose hugs were well-intentioned and full of love, but unfortunately Brooke just wasn't that keen and didn't want her to do it any more.

When my daughter would complain to me, I would ask her why she couldn't tell Emily that she didn't want to be hugged. She would say, 'I don't want to hurt her feelings, Mum. I don't want her to stop being my friend,' and I completely understood her plight.

You see, we're all like Brooke. We aren't awful people who want to put pressure on others or make them feel bad, so sometimes we put other people's needs above our own to keep the peace.

Other reasons we might not assert ourselves include: fear of confrontation; worrying that we will be disliked and rejected; fear of appearing selfish or rude; guilt that we're putting ourselves first; or even the doubt in our own ability to make good decisions.

I truly believe that most people who are passive allow things to happen purely because they don't know *how* to be assertive, or they think of being assertive as a bad thing. Let's be honest, who is teaching us to communicate effectively? I spent a lot of time at school stressing over fractions and the periodic table but, quite honestly, it would have been far more beneficial to teach me how to stand up for myself. But, alas, that's not the case, so let me share with you now one of my own experiences of not being assertive and the reasons behind this.

When I was about 17 and had my first boyfriend, I would stay over at his parents' house all weekend. I have often found myself being independent to a fault and desperately not wanting others to feel they need to do things for me. When I would stay at their house, his lovely and considerate mum would often buzz around me offering food, drinks and anything she could to make my stay pleasant.

I could see that my boyfriend's mum was working hard and so I would often refuse absolutely everything that she offered. Sometimes I'd travelled over two hours to get to their house, so on arrival I was often hungry, tired and dehydrated (I know I'm making it sound like I trekked across a desert, but it was more like a long train journey, and if I were more organised I could definitely have brought snacks...). I refused her offers of refreshments though because I didn't want to 'put her out' or inconvenience her.

When I think back to that time now, I recognise how ludicrous the story was that I was telling myself. In my mind, her knocking me up a ham sandwich was going to trouble her so much that perhaps she wouldn't like me. The truth was that she was really excited to be able to do nice things for me, and allowing her to do so would have given her great joy. If I had recognised the nonsense I was telling myself, I would have been able to assert myself more positively – communicating when I was hungry or thirsty – and I'd have given this thoughtful person the gift of being able to do something nice for someone else.

A note on assertiveness and aggression

Another common reason why people avoid assertiveness is because they confuse it with aggression, and the negative connotations that aggression holds. But the two behaviours are different, as we explored earlier in the chapter. Assertiveness is about confidently stating your wants and needs without bulldozing the wants and needs of others. Aggressiveness, on the other hand, is a triggered and insecure response with no regard for the wants and needs of others. The two should not be confused.

Perhaps, though, you aren't being assertive because you've experienced somebody with high levels of aggression in the past, where standing up for yourself would have resulted in you being on the receiving end of an attack. If this is the case then it makes perfect sense that your clever brain would learn from this, identifying keeping quiet and passive as the safest option in that specific situation.

However, being passive is not the best course of action in every scenario. There are going to be times in life when you are dealing with somebody who is more assertive, more confident and possibly even aggressive, and yet you still have to find ways of asserting yourself. If you have had a bad experience with an aggressive person in the past, it's also important that at some point you start to train your brain that asserting yourself in different situations and with different people will not always result in aggression.

Some of you may also consider aggression as the best way 'to stay safe and get things done' and I promise you there's no judgement here. Again, based on past experiences, this might have served you well. There may have been times in your life when you felt powerless unless you asserted yourself in this more aggressive style. You may also have had caregivers or people around you who dealt with life in this manner, and it's what you learned to do.

Being aggressive may mean that you get your needs met but it will almost definitely mean that others do not. In the long term, it will impair and fracture your relationships, which will in turn impact how you feel. So again, assertion over aggression is the better path.

Nature versus nurture

Just like any traits within our personality, the conversation around
nature versus nurture always comes up: are some people born with
the ability to be assertive, while others are simply not?

Dr Robert Plomin, an American-British psychologist and geneticist,
studied more than 10,000 sets of twins to explore whether our
behaviours are mainly determined at birth or whether learned
behaviours and environment play a bigger part. Although Dr
Plomin didn't study assertiveness directly, he did look at openness,
conscientiousness, extraversion, agreeableness and neuroticism,
and found that these traits were determined by roughly 50 per cent
genetic factors and 50 per cent learned behaviour.

The research therefore shows that even if we have a set amount of
our behaviour and personality fixed at birth, we do still have a huge
chunk that we can play around with and tweak. That's good news
for my less-than-assertive friends because it means that although
it might not come naturally to us, we can *learn* to be assertive, and
that's exactly what I'm going to teach you.

Why does being assertive matter?

Being assertive and getting comfortable with stating what you need
is the surest way of enjoying your life more. Once you crack the code

of being assertive, you'll notice your confidence and self-esteem soar, your relationships prosper and the things that you've been wanting to happen in your life miraculously start materialising.

Last week I had a meeting at my home. Trying to be the dutiful British hostess, I, of course, offered up a warm beverage to my guest. The conversation looked like this:

> Me: 'Would you like a cup of tea, coffee or a cold drink?'
> My guest: 'Whatever you're having.'
> Me: 'I'm having a cup of tea but I'm happy to make you anything that you'd like.'
> My guest: 'Oh, I'll have a cup of tea as well then, please. If that's OK?'
> Me: 'Of course it's OK. How do you take your tea?'

By now I am well aware that I am not dealing with a particularly assertive human. I know that I am in the presence of a beautifully sensitive person who quite clearly doesn't want to put me out in any way. Because of my observations, I have a strong hunch about what the next sentence is going to be.

> My guest: 'Just however it comes.'

This statement is the passive person's mantra of choice. I use this simple example because it highlights so wonderfully that 'just however it comes' hints at how gentle and passive people, like my guest, may deal with many aspects of their lives.

As the host, I know that inside my guest's mind they have a preference. I also know that I'm now going in blind when making their cup of tea. The likely outcome of this wild stab in the dark is that I will make them a cup of tea that they don't enjoy.

'Being assertive and getting comfortable with **stating what you need** is the surest way of **enjoying your life more.**'

Now, of course the stakes are low here. This scenario is not a life-and-death situation, nor will it change either of our lives, but this tiny human interaction is a brilliant way to highlight one conversational style and how to begin changing it if needed.

I made the tea and guessed at my guest's preference. We had our meeting, and I had my cup of black tea, no milk, no sugar, favourite cup, just the way I like it. I enjoyed my drink immensely, but my enjoyment was curtailed as I watched my guest timidly sip at a cup of tea that was very obviously not to their liking.

Nobody is winning in this situation. One person is getting a cup of tea that isn't to their taste and the other feels bad they couldn't give their guest something to make them feel good. Plus, it makes it kind of awkward – it's like there's an elephant in the room that neither of us dares acknowledge.

Let's say we scale this cup of tea debacle to our wider relationships. When we aren't asserting our wants and needs, we keep people at a distance. This might mean that in our romantic relationships or friendships we don't allow people in, and we end up feeling short-changed since they don't fulfil our needs (even though we haven't explained what our needs are in the first place, so how could they possibly do so?).

In order to really connect with people and enjoy a relationship with them, both parties need to feel that they're getting something from it. It's worth learning to say what you want and need without it feeling uncomfortable.

In your working life, not being assertive will affect how successful you are too, and how you are perceived by your peers and your higher-ups. It might mean that you get overlooked for projects because you haven't communicated your desire to be involved or to take on more responsibility. Or you might not get the credit – and rewards – you deserve for the work that you have put in if you stay quiet about your efforts.

Ultimately, there are going to be times in your life when you need to stand up for yourself. You'll need to declare confidently what you want to happen, what you need from other people and potentially even the consequences of these things not happening. There will be moments in your life when you need to set boundaries and say no, and learning to do this in a way that is assertive will increase your chances of getting the things that you want.

So, before going any further, let's remind ourselves of these important facts:

- You have the right to have your needs met.
- You have the right to have your voice heard.
- You have the right to ask for what you want.
- You have the right to ask for time to think.
- You have the right to say no.
- You have the right to disagree.
- You have the right to know why.
- You have the right to be treated with respect and kindness.

The key to being assertive is making sure that you get your needs met by clearly stating what they are. In turn, it's also about ensuring that the people in your world are afforded these same rights to communicate their needs to you. Confident and self-assured people give space for everyone to have their say. As we move to a place where we can deliver clear and direct communication, we must also make space to receive it, too.

Words matter, so watch your chatter

In my first book, *The Happy Me Project: The no-nonsense guide to self-development*, I dedicated a whole chapter to watching what we say to ourselves and the words that come out of our mouths. The reason that it's so important to notice our words is because what we say and think shapes our reality.

The reticular activating system

To explain this a little more, we need to understand how our brains are processing the 4 billion bits of data that they're soaking in each second. If we had to consciously be aware of all of this information, then we would be so overwhelmed we wouldn't be able to function. Thankfully, there is a bundle of nerves at the base of the brainstem called the reticular activating system (RAS) that helps to filter necessary and unnecessary information.

If you were in a shopping centre, for example, and someone said your name, then your RAS would filter out everything else and bring to your attention the person saying your name. Or, if you're an accomplished driver, your RAS no longer needs to offer you every single stimulus involved in driving, but *will* draw your attention to a car pulling in front of you or the red traffic light ahead.

It's important to understand this because the RAS adapts its filtering system to bring to your conscious mind the things that it has deemed important for you to see. Some of this important knowledge is very ingrained and primal, such as when your baby is crying or if there is some form of danger around you.

The brain and the RAS have a strong confirmation bias, though. This means that if you have been focusing on something a lot or have developed a belief about something (good or bad), then your RAS will seek to confirm this belief to be true. I often liken this system to the TikTok algorithm, in that once you're on a certain side of TikTok you are bombarded with videos that match the things you have previously seen and liked.

> **'What we say and think shapes our reality.'**

The RAS, however, doesn't make a distinction about whether something is good or bad for you; it is merely sifting through the data to show you more of what you already believe to be true. This is great news if your beliefs are supportive to you and what you want, but pretty frustrating when they're not.

(As a little aside here, this description of the workings of the brain is based on a neurotypical person and there will be some differences for us non-neurotypical folk. These differences aren't necessarily vast in this case and don't mean you should disregard this explanation. Just be aware of your own unique brain and, as with all of the work we do together, I encourage you to support yourself by listening, learning and understanding your own quirks.)

So, to bring this back to assertiveness: if you currently have some beliefs that you aren't good at being assertive, then your RAS will be looking for more proof of this belief, and possibly for reasons why you shouldn't even try to become assertive.

The good news is that you can change the filtering system of your RAS, and have it start to work in your favour, which is why words matter. The words we repeat to ourselves, either in our minds or out loud, programme our RAS to sift through all the data that we receive and bring to our conscious mind anything that supports our given belief.

Moving from an old belief system to a new one is likely to require some repetition, but if right now you decide that you are going to start using words that support your ability to be assertive, then this is the first step towards getting your RAS on board.

Therefore, I invite you *right now*, from this moment on, to begin declaring loudly: 'I am learning to be assertive.' This way, you are nudging your brain to start reinforcing the message that you *can* and *will* learn to become assertive.

Start to notice the way you talk about yourself. If and when you hear yourself say something that goes against how you would like to be, then STOP, mentally DELETE the phrase, and then REPLACE it with something better. Let's see how this might look in practice:

You: 'I'm just not confident enough to share my opinion.'

STOP.

Mentally DELETE 'I'm just not confident enough to share my opinion.'

REPLACE it with: 'I enjoy sharing my opinions' or 'Each day I get more confident in sharing my opinions.'

Spot the assertive language – an exercise

Before we dive into more tips about assertive language, I want to give you an opportunity to play a little game to see how good you currently are at spotting assertive language. Let me share with you a scenario and then some different responses. For each response, I want you to decide if the response is assertive, passive, passive-aggressive or aggressive.

Scenario 1

You are a manager at work and your employee has made a mistake. You respond:

1 'This piece of work is an absolute mess. There are spelling errors, grammatical errors and I feel embarrassed that this was handed to our client.'

2 'I'm sorry to bring this up, and I'm sure that you didn't mean to do it, but when I was going through your presentation there were a few errors. Please don't worry, though, I make mistakes all the time and it's probably my fault anyway for not checking it before it was sent over to the client. I will apologise to them tomorrow.'

3 'I have noticed that the pieces of work you have handed in recently have had quite a few errors throughout and aren't up to your usual standard. Is there anything I can do to support you, so that this doesn't happen going forward?'

4 'You know, I really do love spending my time rechecking every document that hits my desk. I really don't have anything better to do with my time!'

These four different reactions to an employee handing in substandard work are a great example of how language can be used to change the outcome. How did you get on with labelling each response? I'm confident that you will have guessed that the first example is in the aggressive category, the second is passive, the third is nicely assertive and the fourth is passive-aggressive.

The first example would likely create shame and embarrassment for your employee. It might also create a level of defensiveness in them and make them feel misunderstood. In the second example, the manager takes on the responsibility to fix the problem. This means that the manager is not getting their needs met, as they don't have the work they require from their employee, and the manager will likely continue to get sub-par work handed in to them moving forwards. The third example is an assertive response. It is without judgement and it's direct, concise and compassionate, but with the clear boundary that this cannot continue going forward. The fourth response isn't directed at anyone specifically; it's sarcastic and will leave anyone in the area feeling attacked by your mood, with the 'culprit' likely being none the wiser.

Ready for scenario two? This time, after assigning a communication style to each response, have a go at saying them out loud and notice how each feels.

Scenario 2

Your friend has cancelled on a night out for the third time this month. You respond:

1 'I am so annoyed with you. You're such an idiot. You always do this! You won't be getting invited out ever again.'

2 'No worries. I probably mixed up when it was. It's fine.'

3 'I'm not cross with you. I love getting dressed up for a night out and then sitting on my sofa all night!'

4 'Have you noticed that this is the third time that you have cancelled on me this month? When you cancel it makes me feel like you don't want to spend time with me, or that I've done something to upset you. It also means that I have to move my plans

around at short notice. I value our friendship a great deal but if this happens again, I will have to stop inviting you out.'

Once again, we can see that the first response is overly aggressive. It uses confrontational language, name calling and words like 'always', which is likely to make the other person defensive. This response feels like an attack and is certainly not the open conversation that would allow this friendship to flourish. The second response is passive and will most definitely mean that the friend feels they can cancel on you over and over again until, let's be honest, you either don't speak to the 'canceller' again or you slip right into an aggressive outburst. The third response is once again sarcastic, saying words that imply they aren't upset but being very clear with their tone and body language that they are. None of these outcomes is likely the one you want.

The last example is measured, asks if the person is aware of their behaviour and lets them know how it makes you feel. It reminds them of the importance of the friendship to you, but also asserts a boundary. This will allow the relationship to move forward in a productive way, even if it's an awkward conversation in the short term. (We will keep working throughout this chapter on ways to lessen the feelings of awkwardness, but for now hold in your mind that hard conversations lead to easy lives.)

You see, little language tweaks here and there are often all that it takes to move you from a space of timid and meek to feeling confident in how you speak (the rhyme was not an accident, I will never get bored of rhyming my words!).

Assertive language and how to use it

I want to give you some tangible examples of what assertive language looks and sounds like, so that you can start thinking of ways to bring it into your everyday life. As we go through, I would love you to practise out loud some of the sentences you read and begin noticing how they feel to say.

As you do this, remember that no one is watching you and this is not a test. Let go of the need to be perfect and listen to what thoughts spring to your mind as you try out these phrases. Do you think 'But what if I offend someone?' or 'I feel uncomfortable speaking like this?' Or perhaps you have positive thoughts, such as 'I feel powerful speaking this way' or 'I wonder what changes I could make if I speak like this?' It's OK if you're uncomfortable at this point and if these phrases don't come naturally to you (this will get easier, I promise!).

General rules of being assertive

Let's start with some of the basics when it comes to being assertive:

* **Using 'I' statements** is a really good way to start. So, 'I feel...' or 'I would like...' as opposed to a more aggressive stance of 'You do this...' or 'You make me feel...'. For example, 'When I don't get the opportunity to speak during a meeting, I feel less valued in the team' is likely to get a much better response than 'You never let me speak in the meeting.'
* **Co-operative phrases** like 'What are your thoughts on...?' or 'How does this idea sit alongside your own?' can allow space for collaboration and help foster a better team environment than the more aggressive and demanding stance of 'This is what's going to happen.'
* **Avoid saying 'sorry'** unless you've done something wrong. Hearing 'sorry' peppered throughout a conversation instantly implies that you are more passive in your approach. It will often signal to a more aggressive character that if they push then you will back down.
* **Keep it simple.** Be clear, concise and direct.

Addressing 'bad behaviour' in an assertive (not aggressive) manner

Here are my favourite techniques for addressing bad behaviour assertively:

I notice, I interpret, am I right?

This is one of my favourite ways of addressing somebody's irritating, inappropriate or ill-thought-out behaviour without it spiralling into an argument. You are stating that you have noticed a particular behaviour, that you are interpreting it in a particular way and then you are asking for clarification. This allows the person to not feel like they are being attacked (because they're not) but also lets them know that you have noticed their behaviour and are asking for more of an explanation.

'**I notice** that you are often late for our Friday work meeting. **I interpret** that to mean that you don't particularly want to be at the meeting. **Am I right?**'

Make use of questions

'Really, that's interesting, can you tell me more?'

'When did this last happen?'

'What is the evidence to support this?'

If you find yourself in a position where somebody is verbally attacking you, then try responding with a question, such as one of the examples above. This technique allows the person to have the space they need to get out what they want to say. Plus, it can also have the benefit of letting them run out of steam *and* giving you time to think.

You can also use questions to get a person to admit their bad behaviour on their own. For example, you could ask, 'How many times this month do you think you have cancelled our lunch dates?' This is not you saying, 'You always cancel our lunch dates!', which will almost certainly get a negative response. Using a question allows and encourages the person to self-reflect.

Pointing out the process

This is where you point out what you can see. The benefit of this is that it enables the person to notice from somebody else's perspective what is going on. Of course, you won't always get the response you want, but it's a great tool to have in your belt: to state what you see and assert what you feel is going on.

This might look like, 'I can tell by your response that you feel very angry about this' or 'I can see from your body language that you are unhappy with this situation.'

One of my coaching clients shared that every time she visited her family home, her mum would say, 'Long time no see, you barely come round here anymore.' This instantly made my client feel bad and not want to go round to her mum's again. My client practised pointing out the process after her mum dropped her usual 'long time no see' line, and said, 'Mum, every time I come round here you complain that I don't come round here enough.' This allowed her mum to notice her behaviour. My client then went on to explain how that made her feel and they worked on their relationship from there.

I know it can sometimes be difficult to change the habitual language that we use (especially with those closest to us), so I really encourage you to look at the challenging situations you regularly encounter and pre-prepare some assertive phrases that you could try in these scenarios. It's important that you craft these tangible sentences in advance so that you can practise beforehand (and practising is non-negotiable).

From passive to assertive language

Now let's look at more ways we can go from passive to assertive in the words that we say and also *how* we are saying them. Remember, even if (right now) these phrases feel very alien in their directness, with practice you'll start to find them easier. Also, when you begin to see the benefits of assertiveness in your life, it might just get a bit addictive (based on both my clients' experiences and my own!). Try practising saying the following phrases out loud:

Instead of saying, 'I just want to talk about...'
Say, 'I want to talk about...'

Instead of saying, 'Does that make sense?'
Say, NOTHING. (It makes sense.)

Instead of saying, 'I'm so sorry for bothering you but I need a response to that email by midday.'
Say, 'I need a response to that email by midday.'

Instead of saying, 'I could be wrong.'
Say, 'I believe...'

Instead of saying, 'This is probably stupid but...'
Say, 'I have a unique idea...'

Instead of saying, 'If it's OK with everyone I would like to...'
Say, 'This is what I believe needs to happen.'

It's not only the words we say that matter when it comes to being assertive though, it's also *how* we say them. If we mumble the words under our breath, for example, then we're unlikely to come across as assertive and get the reaction that we hoped for.

It's also worth noting that there can be a difference in terms of the written word versus the spoken word and it can be a particular challenge to get the balance right when writing. My rule of thumb is to keep emails as short and sharp as possible. Aim to be empathetic without slipping into a deep dive of apologetic language; offer context for what you're saying and an explanation as to why; give clear direction on what you want and end with the normal warm language you would normally use.

Remember to proofread your writing. Take out any unnecessary caps on words or aggressive double exclamation marks. At the end of reading through, you may decide that it's better to have this conversation in person or on a video call to avoid misunderstandings.

Assertive speakers make themselves heard. They slow down when they speak (because confident people know that others will wait for what they have to say); they communicate what they want or need in a direct fashion; and their shoulders are often back, taking up space, with an open posture.

Avoiding 'upspeak'

There is a phenomenon that is commonly referred to as 'upspeak' (a term first coined by journalist James Gorman in a 1993 *New York Times* article), and it refers to when somebody has a rising inflection at the end of a factual sentence. You often hear it in certain accents – for example, it's highly prevalent in America and Australia (and I know this because my daughter insists on listening to American and Australian YouTubers at decibels you'd expect at Glastonbury...). Upspeak can make statements sound like they are questions, and when used too frequently it can sound to the listener as though the person lacks confidence.

Let me give you an example statement that you can try out, with and without an inflection. Perhaps even record yourself saying it and then listen back.

Statement to be read as a fact: 'The day was a huge success.'

Statement to be read as a question: 'The day was a huge *success*?'

When you make a statement sound like a question, it can appear like you're asking for permission or that you don't truly believe what you are saying. When you're going to have conversations in which you need to be assertive, this is one to watch out for and avoid.

Now we've had a look at some practical speaking tips, I want to delve back into the internal stuff again because, let's be honest, it's the internal stuff that's running the show.

You can't be everyone's favourite flavour (and you don't need to be)

In the USA, ice cream is an 8-billion-dollar industry. Eight billion dollars on ice cream! Wow. That is some big money spent on those sundaes and, in my opinion (and clearly many other people's too), it sounds like money well spent.

Ice cream, we can say with good authority, is making nearly everyone happy (and I know this is a broad statement, don't come for me my dairy-free or ultra-processed food-avoiding friends!).

There are of course many different flavours of ice cream and not everyone is going to like the same type. Some people prefer classic vanilla, some try something different each time, and some even act as though enjoying coffee ice cream is perfectly normal behaviour...! (I joke, of course, you can like whatever you wish, but I'll have a mint choc chip please, if you're buying.)

So why are we talking about ice cream? Well, if we reflect this concept back to us as people, we might notice that some of us are trying to be liked by *everyone*. We're trying to be everyone's favourite ice cream flavour, even though that's simply not possible.

People pleasing

The trait of trying to be liked by everyone is referred to as people pleasing. This is not a diagnosis, but a personality trait recognised by psychologists. A people pleaser is a person who puts everyone else's needs before their own and will spend much of their day-to-day life trying to be what everyone else needs them to be.

It comes with a feeling of wanting to fit in and belong. People pleasers, who could well be your best friends, mother-in-law, favourite employee or *you*, may under the surface be struggling with feelings of low self-esteem. Our worry that people might not like us and that we may be pushed out of the group is such an ingrained concern for our brains' survival mode that it can have us doing anything to fit in (*see* p. 37 for more detail on this).

It does appear that a lot of people-pleasing behaviours seem more prevalent in women, but men are not immune to this behaviour either. The desire to be popular and liked by all can become such a strong pull for some of us that the idea of being confident and assertive in who we are and what we can offer feels completely alien.

The truth is, though, that just like a certain ice cream flavour, not everyone is going to like you and you can't fight that. That's actually a nice thought, because it means you don't have to work as hard;

you can just be your own perfect flavour and some people are going to totally love that.

A word of warning – as you begin to do the work and start asserting your own needs, it will mean that some people don't get to have you at their beck and call any more, which some might not like. Perhaps you stop saying yes to helping the parent and teacher association (PTA) and get a few pushy WhatsApp messages* about how they really need someone to run the cake stall (stand firm, my friend, stand firm!).

Or perhaps when you assert to your boss that you won't be taking your laptop on holiday this time and she drops a passive-aggressive 'Well let's hope we can meet the August deadline prior to that then' it might make you feel so sick with worry that you consider cancelling the holiday (don't!).

Ugh, I know that doesn't feel too great, does it? Let's take a moment here to acknowledge that feeling of worry, fear or anxiety that you have let people down or they might be annoyed at you because you've asserted yourself. It can feel scary, can't it? The thing is though, you're here because you want to get your needs met and you want to have real and honest connections with people, and in order to do that there will be a little discomfort at first. Stick with it though, breathe through the tricky bits and you'll come out the other side feeling so happy that you did.

To help you, let me paint a picture of what happens when we try to be liked by all.

That friend calls to see if you could babysit this weekend and you say, 'Yes.' Your boss asks you to stay later and you say, 'Of course.'

---

* Perhaps these 'pushy' mums are actually trying to be assertive, but have slipped into the passive-aggressive rants we have been discussing.

Your husband asks if you could cook for him and his friends and you say, 'I'll sort it.' You don't want to let anyone down and find yourself rushing from work (having stayed an hour later) straight to the supermarket to pick up food for your husband and his friends. You barely get a second to go to the toilet before jumping in the car to babysit your friend's kids.

Everyone thinks you're amazing but you're thoroughly depleted.

As a one-off, it's no big deal. But if you find yourself saying yes constantly because you're not sure how to assert boundaries and say no, then you and I need to do some work.

Setting boundaries

Asserting boundaries, especially with those we care about, or with those in a more senior role to us at work, is something I revisit monthly in The Happy Me Project community. We do this regularly because so many of us find this hard. But boundary setting is essential when standing up for ourselves and asserting our needs.

Identifying your boundaries

Let's first take a gander at where we can have boundaries and explore what yours are or what you would *like* them to be.

Intellectual boundaries
This is about respect for everyone's ideas and viewpoints even when ours differ, e.g. 'I respect the fact that we have different political views and for the sake of a nice family dinner, let's agree to disagree and not discuss politics.'

Emotional boundaries

This is your right to be respected and have your emotional needs met. This might look like saying, 'I don't like it when you discuss my weight in front of the family' or 'I don't feel comfortable talking about this right now.'

Material/financial boundaries

This may look like saying, 'I don't lend money to anyone' or 'Please don't borrow my clothes without asking.'

Sexual boundaries

Quite simply, your right to consent, to say no, to state what your likes and dislikes are, e.g. 'That is not something I am comfortable with.'

Physical boundaries

This includes your physical self, e.g. 'I don't do hugs', and your physical space, e.g. 'I don't allow people to smoke in my home.'

Religious/spiritual boundaries

This might look like saying, 'I pray every morning before anything else' or 'Sunday is reserved for going to church.'

Time boundaries

This focuses on how you wish to allocate your time, e.g. 'I don't take work calls on weekends. I reserve this for family time.'

Non-negotiable boundaries

These are your own non-negotiables and can look like anything from saying, 'Mum, I won't be bringing the kids round to your house while your dog is allowed to run around freely' to 'I don't accept any kind of infidelity in relationships.'

Take some time to decide what your boundaries are by reflecting on the list above. Are some very relatable to you? Perhaps you've experienced conflict in these areas previously?

How to set your boundaries

Next, it's time to think about how to vocalise your boundaries to those around you, in an assertive and confident fashion. Let's explore this:

Thanks + your boundary

'I appreciate you caring enough to offer advice, but I have enough information now.'

Understanding + your boundary

'I know this is going to be difficult for you to hear but I won't be coming to your BBQ while Uncle John is there.'

Schedule change + your boundary

'I don't have time to help you paint your living room this week, but I'd be happy to help you next week.'

Help + your boundary

'I am too busy to take anything more on right now, but I can forward your contact details to someone else who might be able to help.'

Cut-off + your boundary

'I don't feel like I am being respected in this conversation and so I'm going to end the call.'

Your feelings + your boundary

'I feel upset and let down when you talk about me to other people and if that continues then I won't be able to share anything with you at all.'

Remember that you can choose to say no to anything that you wish to say no to, and you can also ask for more time to make your decision: 'Let me come back to you' can be a great way to give yourself a moment to think. It can also give you time to prepare yourself to say no or to assert how you'd like something done a different way. There may be times in your life when you'd like to say no but your wider values have you saying yes, such as when caring for a sick loved one. That is still a choice you're making because it feels important to you.

If people ignore your boundaries

We also need to know that if we create a boundary and someone steps their big boots over that boundary, what the consequence of that is.

When I think about this, I'm reminded of my mum telling me she would 'never let her dog on her sofa'. A bold and assertive statement you might think, but when the winter nights drew in and a cold wind blew outside her home, that boundary became as solid as a paper wall. Up popped the dog, snuggled into a blanket and loving his life. The next day, guess where she found the dog? Yep, snuggled back up on the sofa, totally unaware that any boundary existed.

Since dogs don't speak, relaying consequences for boundary breaking is a little more challenging to assert (!) but in our human lives, communicating the consequences of breaking a boundary is an important part of establishing it in the first place. For example, we might say, 'Every time I come to your house you discuss my relationship status and I don't like it. If you continue to do this, then I will stop coming round.'

The slightly more challenging side to this is that you have to follow through with the consequence if they continue the behaviour. Nine times out of 10 the assertive sentence that states the consequence is often enough to get them to see that their behaviour is unacceptable and it encourages change. If they happen to be the one who ignores it though, and they push your boundary another time, then implementing the consequence is not only the right response

'Ultimately, you can sit in a space of being a people pleaser and not having your needs met or **you can have boundaries;** you can't have both.'

but it sounds to me that they're likely not the type of person you need in your life anyway.

Ultimately, you can sit in a space of being a people pleaser and not having your needs met or you can have boundaries; you can't have both. This doesn't mean you become cold and unkind, it's about balance, fairness and standing up for yourself.

I'm ready to be an assertive badass, where do I start?

To help you put into practice the techniques we've discussed in this chapter, here are some action points to get you started.

Inside:

1 **Create a sense of calm.** Before being assertive, take in some nice, full, intentional breaths. As you do, add in some affirming mantras to indicate to your brain how you would like things to go (yep, we even need to get assertive with our own brains!). Three mantras to get you started could be: 'My voice matters', 'My feelings are valid' and 'I am in control of how I show up.' Say them out loud as often as you can.

2 **Write a list of your personal boundaries.** Look back to the list of boundaries on p. 96. Next to each relevant one, decide on a boundary and write out some assertive boundary-setting sentences for you to practise out loud (see p. 97 for help with these). If your internal people-pleaser tendency is being triggered to accept less, go back to the beginning of this chapter and re-read your 'rights' until the people pleaser within is silenced. Practise setting and putting

into action one or two of those personal boundaries this week, starting small and gradually working your way through your list to those bigger ones.

3 Visualise being assertive. Think about a scenario you've been in before or that you see coming up in the future and picture yourself within this scene as your best assertive self. In your mind's eye, imagine what you see, and how the other person is behaving. Notice your posture, tone, gestures and the words you are using. See the effect of this confidence and notice how it makes you feel. I visualise like this every night and when it's time to do it in real life, my brain knows what to do.

Outside:

1 Stand your ground. In certain circumstances, this might be both literally and figuratively, but when we are thinking about body language and your outside self, I'm talking about grounding yourself where you are. This means adopting an open posture, putting your shoulders back, maintaining eye contact and having your hands on show. If you are sitting, stay sitting. If you are standing, stay standing. An assertive person with gravitas and confidence isn't darting around or bobbing up and down. Plant your feet on the ground and be intentional about your movements.

2 Slow down your speech. When you speak slower and at a lower pitch, you draw people in, and you give the impression that you are in control of a situation. If the other person is speaking fast or even aggressively, slowing down your speech will imply that you have the upper hand in that conversation and it may have the added bonus of slowing them down too and bringing a more peaceful resolution to the conversation. Practise playing with the speed of your delivery over the next week (at work, with your children and even with your pets).

3 **Role play.** OK, OK, I know that some of you just saw 'role play' and had a visceral reaction to it. Maybe you've had to do some awful role-playing at work and it brings back some hideously embarrassing experience, but bear with me. Practice makes perfect and practising daily scenarios in which you would need to be assertive is going to be beneficial in building your confidence. I have put together a printout of scenarios for you to try with a trusted friend or family member, which you can access on my website. The idea is to practise your assertive sentences, with all the associated confident body language to go with it. Here are a few examples to get you started: telling a waiter there's a problem with your food; saying no to someone asking you for a favour; and telling someone that you don't like a word that they're using (I had this recently with someone using an ableist slur that they didn't know was no longer used).

Guest advice

Jefferson Fisher
Personal injury lawyer who helps people argue less, so they can talk more
@jefferson_fisher / @justaskjefferson

❝The first thing I advise is knowing *when* to stand up for yourself. Not everyone is worth getting out your chair for. It is a "know your worth" mentality. Just because they spew out trash doesn't mean we are in the business of digging through garbage.❞

#4

Trying something new

I was recently interviewed for a podcast called *The Creative Switch*. This is a show hosted by Nikki Vallance, a coach and author whose audience are looking to move from a more traditional and corporate way of working into the Wild West of creative pursuit and being freelance. The people who follow Nikki's work (much like Nikki herself) have or are in the process of starting something new and following a different path to the one they, or perhaps those around them, expected of them.

This bravery excites me more than perhaps it should. The driving factor in so much of what I do is the belief that life is short (whether you hold beliefs about there being another level to existence or not). Your time on this planet should therefore be lived in a way that excites and thrills you, and you can decide to explore this at any point.

The problem I find (and maybe you sit in this space) is that people are often scared to start something new. They're worried about failing, fearful of looking stupid, or doubtful of their own abilities. The result of this uncertainty is that their feet remain firmly nailed to the floor, and they stay in the same place.

Unfortunately, what then happens over time is that under this fear and doubt grows the feeling of being unfulfilled. The mundaneness of life starts to suffocate us and we can even begin to resent those around us for 'making' us stay where we are. We might also find ourselves pouring scorn on the 'courageous ones' who took the leap you wish you had.

This depressing tale of regret doesn't have to be your story (even if it sounds a lot like the current reality). You haven't missed the boat and you're not too old. If Helen Mirren can pick up an Oscar at the age of 61, Gladys Burrill can run a marathon and set a Guinness World Record for the oldest female marathon finisher at the age of 92, and Peter Roget can publish the first ever thesaurus at the age of 73 (thank you Pete, I am a fan of your work), then *you* can do whatever you want!

In this chapter, we're going to learn how to 'break through to the new', 'mesh with the fresh' and something that rhymes with 'have fearless confidence to pursue all of our madcap goals and ideas.' We'll begin by exploring the psychology of newness, then part one will focus on 'being new', part two will look at 'trying something new', and in part three we'll delve into any limiting beliefs you might have and make a plan for how to replace 'em. Ready? Let's go.

The psychology behind new and unchartered territory

Trying something new comes with a whole load of uncertainty and our brains are wired to hate this. Every day, our brains are updating our software to be aware of any potential new information that we might need and any new threats to our survival. It's always on the lookout to work out what is safe and what is not. Anything new, without all the questions answered, feels uncertain and our brains will see this as a danger.

This is the exact reason why we often overreact to things that might be considered fairly gentle activities, such as going on holiday. I can't be the only person who, on occasion, has made prepping for a package holiday to Brit fave Tenerife feel ridiculously challenging. I mean, dramatic isn't even the word.

'Your time on this planet should be lived in a way that **excites** and **thrills** you.'

As I run through the 3 billion items on my holiday checklist, meticulously crossing off my (completely over-the-top) list of 'essentials' for a week's hang-out by the pool, my poor brain is desperately trying to stay within the confines of what it knows and what it can be sure of.

This means that trying a new dish at your local take-away, starting a new job or even experimenting with a new haircut can feel risky and unsettling, and it often means that we don't actually do any of these things.

In the short term, sticking with what we know will feel better than stepping out of our comfort zones, but long term, this will feel utterly terrible as you watch your 'dream life' become exactly that. You'll then wish you'd dared to defy your brain's hardwiring and taken a chance.

Research from a UCL study proved that we would rather feel physical pain than live with uncertainty. In the study, test subjects were either told they had a 50 per cent chance of receiving an electric shock or a 100 per cent chance of receiving one. They found that those who knew for certain they would get the shock remained calmer and more able to deal with the outcome compared to those who were unsure. The lead author of the study, Archy de Berker, concluded that we find uncertainty uncomfortable: 'It turns out that it's much worse not knowing you're going to get a shock than knowing you definitely will or won't.'

Sticking with what we know in life limits our uncertainty, which is why so many of us stay doing things we're not happy with, rather than risk change and the unknown. But certainty and safety and simply staying alive does not equal a fabulous life. So, muster the courage to rebel against this programmed response – and try something new – is where we're going to focus our attention in this chapter.

Part 1: being new

I put on the navy blue jumper and checked my hair in the mirror. I'd just made my mum iron my naturally wavy hair on the ironing board so it was poker straight at the bottom and wavy on top (a plight that future generations will never understand). I was 14 and just a few months earlier had begged my parents to let me move from the secondary school I was attending to a completely different school, a 20-minute bus ride away.

Today was my first day and the 'what if' butterflies looped my stomach as I cautiously boarded the bus. This wasn't the first time I'd been the new girl somewhere and I'd grown pretty good at dealing with the challenging feelings that can arise from being new. I had even begun to like the new interactions as it felt like a clean slate – an opportunity to introduce myself as the most recent version of myself, without the baggage of what was. Sometimes a new environment can help you give yourself permission to be who you know you are, but perhaps have held back from being elsewhere for fear of judgement.

Within minutes of arriving at my new school I was almost surrounded by inquisitive students wanting to know who this new girl was and why she was joining after the school year had started. I have to applaud my parents for allowing me to move from where I was (a place I wasn't doing so well at emotionally) because being a parent of a hormonal teenage girl was new to them too, so I'm very grateful they listened to me.

On this particular first day I was awash with feelings and thoughts that you might be familiar with from various points in your own life. These included the worries of not knowing where anything was or who anyone was, the awkwardness of who to sit with at lunch or break, but most importantly, my brain was desperately trying to predict and work out what would happen next with all of this uncertainty around me.

After leaving school, we might get lulled into believing that our days as the new kid are over, but they're simply just getting started. Think about how often you might be the new one in a situation. It could be starting a new job, attending a new class, joining a new sports team or being the new parent on the school drop-off treadmill. It might be joining a new friendship group or getting a new partner, who then introduces you to their friends and family. You'll be the new neighbour, new volunteer, new to the department ... and the cycle will continue until you're the eccentric, new old person doddering around the nursing home.

That being the case, I think we'd better make sure that we're armed with the tools we need to feel as confident as possible when navigating the newbie role.

Strategies for being new

Fears or anxieties about being new can arise for all of us. It doesn't matter about your background, your job title or how cool and confident you are in one area of your life. It's perfectly normal to have niggling fears about being new, so we'll first look at strategies that you can use to support yourself as a newbie in any situation.

The positives of being 'new'

Let's begin by considering what's appealing about being new. This is important because if we confront new experiences head-on with optimism, excitement and a firm understanding of what they have to offer us, then we'll find any uncomfortable moments during the process far easier to navigate. Here are some examples of how being new can be positive:

- It provides the chance to make new friends.
- It brings opportunities for career progression in a new company.
- It offers the chance to start afresh and explore the most up-to-date depiction of ourselves.
- New challenges can ignite a sense of purpose.
- New experiences can spark our creativity.
- It gives us a chance to introduce boundaries and rules we may have found hard to put in place with people who have known us longer.
- There may be new opportunities to learn a new skill.
- New physical challenges such as joining a sports team might help us to test our physical boundaries and unleash new energy.
- Going somewhere new can help us see the world from a different perspective as we might be mixing with different crowds or understanding different cultures.

- New hobbies may help us find a new way to socialise or relax.
- Trying something new or visiting a new place with friends or family can be a very connecting experience.
- It affords the often-missed opportunity to start a cool new nickname for yourself. (When my husband joined a hospital ward as a new patient, he tried to convince his team that his nickname was 'Buffalo Soldier'. He even had them write it on the whiteboard above his bed. His nickname didn't catch on, but maybe yours will.)

Ultimately, new experiences and situations push us out of a rut – away from the monotony and relentlessness of life – and help us to feel alive. I don't know about you, but this list has me chomping at the bit to be the new kid in class.

Gather knowledge

Now that we've been reminded of the positives of being new, it's time to gather as much information about the situation as possible. This includes: where you're going, how you'll get there, who you'll be meeting and what you'll be doing when you get there. Finding certainties among the unknown is very reassuring, so familiarise yourself with whatever is available to help you feel more in control.

Today, there is a vast amount of accessible information online, so make the most of it. This might include being able to see the person you're meeting on social media. Now, a word of warning: don't go five years deep into someone's history, liking and commenting as you go, or there's a high chance they'll see you as an unhinged stalker. But a cursory glance to check what they look like, so they feel familiar and you recognise them, will be just fine. You could also look at the Street View footage of where you're heading to check out the parking situation or the nearest bus stop. Perhaps you can find pictures of the space you'll be visiting so you can familiarise yourself with the layout. Or a TikTok or Instagram video might offer a review of what you're about to do, for example if you're trying a new exercise class.

'Remember that you **don't have to be perfect**. Enjoy the newbie freedom to make permissible mistakes because **being new means zero expectation is placed on you**.'

Take off the pressure

Remember that you don't have to be perfect. Enjoy the newbie freedom to make permissible mistakes because being new means zero expectation is placed on you (yay!). Perhaps you go into the wrong room, don't have the right sports kit or call someone the wrong name. It's no biggie, you're new!

Stay open in your mind and body language – smile, be warm and engage with those whom you meet – but you're not expected to know everything so don't be scared to ask questions that clarify or explain. 'Would it be possible for you to take me on a tour so I can get to know where everything is?', 'Is there a list of equipment and uniform I will need for this class?' and 'Could you please send me a list of everyone's names and job titles, so I can make sure I'm getting things to the right people and can get to know everyone?' are just a few examples of perfectly reasonable newbie questions.

Take note of the 'liking gap'

A study conducted by the Association for Psychological Science discovered something that is now called the 'liking gap'. This is the gap between our perception of how much someone likes us and the reality. Essentially, this study found that we aren't very good at working out how much a person we've chatted with likes us, and if our inner voice is particularly critical, this makes the gap bigger. With the noise of our inner critic telling us we're foolish and awkward, we may well miss any signals given off by the other person that they're enjoying our company. We therefore could run on the (incorrect) assumption that they must feel as critically about us as we do. So, have this study in mind if your brain tries to convince you that everyone hates you as you venture out into a new part of the world.

Strategies for being new – specific scenarios

Now let's combine what we've just discussed with some tips for more specific new-person scenarios that so many of us face.

New job

- Plan your journey and get there early so you feel calm on arrival.
- Be proactive in seeking knowledge from your managers and peers by asking questions when you're unsure of something. 'How do you prefer to communicate, in person or by email?' 'Who are the key people whom you think I should make contact with?' Or even the more basic information, such as 'Do I need a parking pass?' Get these questions out early, so you feel confident as you move forward.
- Build relationships by making an effort to get to know your colleagues. Could you ask a few people out for a coffee or sit with them at lunch? This will help you to settle in quicker and feel part of the gang, and it'll mean you'll have more people whom you can ask for help when needed.
- Listen and observe. This can help you to understand your environment more, assess the dynamic of the space, understand the relationships between people, and make sure you're not missing information that will help you in the early days.
- Be adaptable and flexible. Remain open to challenges and prepare your mind for the potential that things may be different to how you've imagined them.
- Ask for feedback at an appropriate point (if this is a challenge, there's more advice about this on p. 151). Hearing that you're on track will help build your confidence. If there are things you can improve on then ask for support to do this and have confidence in the fact that you're being proactive and taking control.

New to the class

- Walk into the class with your head held high, looking to grab eye contact and offer a smile to people as you enter.
- Be a beginner even if you've taken a class similar to this before. Allow yourself to remain receptive to learning.
- Befriend the one who knows everyone. This person can likely give you the low-down on the class dynamics, how it runs and all the hacks to improve your chances of success.

- If you have questions or need guidance, ask the instructor or teacher. Don't be afraid to have no idea what you're doing.

New to the school run

- Remember that every parent in the school playground was at some point new and unsure of how things worked, so they get it.
- Be compassionate to yourself about any emotional attachment you may have to your child getting older and going to school. Not everyone finds this easy, and the flood of those feelings might impact your ability to assess how 'well' you're doing socially.
- Have your head up and shoulders back and challenge yourself to engage with a couple of people each day. Try a smile, a 'good morning' or a chat about the school trip the kids are going on soon. Practice makes perfect and you might well help someone else feel more at ease as a bonus.

New neighbour

- Knock on your new neighbours' doors and introduce yourself.
- Ask about them and listen with interest.
- Learn about your new local area and any neighbourhood knowledge that would support you. Are there any local events or even (God forbid!) a committee you could join? (You might be in a committee, love the committee or run the committee, so you do you, but just please don't add me to the WhatsApp group.)
- Be as you'd like them to be with you. If you want a good neighbour, start by showing up as one.

New to the family/friendship group

- Remind yourself that the people you're about to meet love the person who is introducing you, so they are already set up to like you!
- Wear your 'most you' outfit. There's something about wearing the clothes that make you feel the most yourself that has you entering new spaces with a tad more swagger. Plus, in this instance, it's way better to leave any pretence at the door because you probably want these people to get to know the real you.

- Be interested in others. You don't have to have a monologue prepared but get to know them. If you ask questions and allow them to speak, research from a Harvard University study tells us that this will make them like you more.

Part 2: starting something new

From 2020 to 2021, a staggering 726,000 new start-up businesses opened in the UK, with March 2021 showing the biggest increase seen since HMRC records began in 1989. When we see the numbers of those new start-ups on a page it's easy to separate them from actual people and real lives, but let's try to remember that each of those numbers is a person taking a leap of faith, perhaps for the first time in their lives. To me, those numbers represent a whole heap of guts, grit and mettle.

Now, of course, some of those businesses were probably started purely because some people were bored during those pandemic years, and it's also possible that many of those businesses are no longer operational as you read this book.

However, there were many people during this period who were forced out of their jobs due to redundancy and decided to become self-employed. There were also those who used the chaos of the pandemic as the opportunity to finally jump ship from a job they didn't enjoy to begin the business they'd always dreamed about.

A good friend of mine, James Keith (or JK as he is known to his mates) was among this cohort. During the upheaval of 2020 he was made redundant from a well-paid and seemingly secure job. With a young daughter and bills still needing to be paid, this was a huge blow and one he did nothing to deserve.

It would have been easy for JK to panic after receiving this news, and to have hurriedly jumped into any company that would have him.

Instead, he paused and took a moment to reflect. The lockdown and lack of socialising gave JK the quiet time he needed to really consider his work options and consider what he'd ideally love to do.

With a background in marketing and a desire to create something, JK took the brave and uncertain step to set up his own business. Awesomesauce Marketing burst on to the scene in mid-2020 and, within the year, it was expanding to a second office. The leap of faith had paid off.

Although there will always be challenges along the way, this is a prime example of how getting comfortable with fresh starts (even when it feels scary and you didn't ask for one), can be the difference between enduring a life that is forced upon you and enjoying a life where you build your own future and create your own rules.

JK's story is a positive one and it was fascinating to see so many people using the pandemic as a springboard to begin something new. But you don't need to wait for a global pandemic to boot you into action! You can start something new at any time. In fact, we start here, we start now and in the next section I will be giving you the toolkit to do so.

How to start something new – the toolkit

This exercise is for those crossroad moments in our life. The times when you know you want change and to shake things up, but you're not really sure what that looks like for you. You feel stuck but don't know where to turn. It's also for those of you who do have a goal in mind but don't know how to flesh it out and turn it into a plan. You feel stuck. If this is you, then go grab a cuppa, get a pen and paper and let's start doing some exploring.

Step one – new ideas for change

On a sheet of paper, I want you to brain dump any ideas for change that have ever crossed your mind. For example, 'I want to open a bakery', 'I would love to learn to roller skate' or 'I want to finally pass my driving test.' You're not going to filter these *at all* and it's not for anyone else to see. Dump 'em down, the crazier the better (yep, that one thought that just snuck into your mind, stop shielding it and get it down on paper).

If you're stuck for ideas, consider the different areas of your life and what you'd improve or change if fear and money didn't (currently) feel like blockers. This might be that you want to change your environment or your work life, maybe you want to feel better about your outward appearance or you want to improve your relationship with your partner. Perhaps it's specific things, such as 'I want to move to Australia' or 'I've always wanted to train to be a nurse.' They don't all have to be huge changes either; perhaps it's 'I want to go to the cinema on my own', 'I want to dye my brown hair blonde' or 'I want to put up the shelves in the spare room.'

You might want to think about change across all aspects of your life in one go. Or perhaps you'd like to focus on one area of your life at a time. You could start by focusing purely on your home, your relationship or another singular choice, and then revisit this exercise again, when you're ready, and focus on another area.

If you need some inspiration, check out the list of suggested topics below:

- Your home
- Your family
- Your work
- Your education
- Your appearance
- Your health
- Your relationships
- Your heart, soul, passion, purpose (or whatever word sparks thoughts)

The choice is yours in terms of how you'd like to approach this brain dump. I suggest you play around with it and don't overthink it. You'll be amazed at how many ideas for change float to the surface when you get started – go with it!

Step two – what makes you happy?

Now you have a list of all your wonderful ideas for change, it's time to look inwards. To do this I invite you to reach for a second piece of paper and think about the following questions:

- What brings you joy in life?
- What has made you happy in the past?
- When do you feel at peace?
- What helps you to feel a sense of purpose and connection to the world?

Your answers might look like:

- 'I felt happy when I cooked dinner for my friends last week.'
- 'I always love playing squash with my dad.'
- 'I enjoy it when I'm feeling challenged at work.'
- 'I feel good about myself when I'm exercising regularly.'
- 'Staying on top of my laundry and housework makes me feel calm.'
- 'Having a financial budget in place with my partner makes me feel in control and gives me peace.'
- 'My job as a care worker gives me a sense of purpose.'

Again, don't overthink this. At this stage we're simply acknowledging the 'ingredients' in life that bring you happiness and peace.

Step three – choose your next move

Gather together your two pieces of paper: your list of new ideas for creating change in your life and your list of things that bring you happiness and peace.

Looking at both sets of notes together, it's time to choose something new to try. Go for something from the first list of new ideas that aligns with the things you know make you happy, as recorded in the second list. For example, let's look at two (very short!) sets of lists, below:

List 1 – new ideas:
- 'I want a kitchen like the girl I follow on YouTube has.'
- 'I want to go on a walking holiday.'
- 'I want to train to become a yoga instructor.'

List 2 – ways I feel happiness and peace:
- 'I love getting out into nature.'
- 'I love having a tidy, organised home.'
- 'Doing yoga is my peaceful space.'

With the lists above, we could begin thinking about these as follows. We know that if you chose to renovate your tired kitchen, inspired by a girl on YouTube, then this would align with you having a tidy and organised home, which you've identified makes you happy. If you chose to begin researching a walking holiday then you also know this would help you feel good because being outside in nature is something that brings you joy. Likewise, training to be a yoga instructor could be a good move for you because having yoga in your life brings you a sense of peace. Working through your two lists together will hopefully help you hone in on the new ideas to try that will bring you the most joy in your life.

A disclaimer: I know that choosing something new to try might be a challenge for some of you (I am you). Perhaps having everything written down may feel overwhelming. So stop. Take a breath. Take the pressure off. We're just playing and exploring here. Take five minutes, get outside for a bit of fresh air, then try again. If you come back to this and you're still finding it a lot, then give yourself permission to come back another day.

Another step to combat overwhelm is to take the pressure off with the knowledge that our choices aren't permanent. We might choose to do something only once, and that's OK. For example, we might choose to 'take a tap class', 'spend an afternoon writing a children's book' or 'cook a new dish every week'. If we don't enjoy it, we choose again. If this happens, it's still a win. It means you've tried something new, learned something, and the lesson in this instance is that the change we tried is not the change we want. This is all part of the process. There's no loss in trying something new and deciding it's not for you; there is only loss in not trying at all. If you change nothing, nothing changes, and if you try nothing, you stay exactly where you are.

> **'There's no loss in trying something new and deciding it's not for you; there is only loss in not trying at all.'**

Step four – take action

When you've decided on something new to try, it's helpful to immediately decide on one action step to move this forward. Make this the easiest one possible. If you decide you want to go on a walking holiday then perhaps your first action point is to ask your colleague where they went on their walking holiday last year. Easy. If you decide to cook a new dish every week then perhaps your first step is to find a few recipes you like the look of online and print them off or screenshot them. If you choose to become a yoga instructor then the first step might be to book yourself on a course. Or the step might be even smaller still – it could be to ring your yoga teacher and ask them where they trained.

These may feel like minor steps forward, and the perfectionists among us might be tempted to overhaul everything immediately, but try to hold back. For many people, if we do too much at once then we will likely burn out and soon become demotivated and daunted by the task right at the beginning. Take things slow. I want you to enjoy the process, and starting small allows you to get an instant win as you tick off your first step.

Ultimately, when we have no clue what we want but we know that it's not *this,* then doing something, doing anything, while moving towards action is the most important step. The motivation will ebb and flow in our lives, but action will create more action and staying still will have you trying to 'will' yourself to find some big life purpose (while barely being able to get off the sofa). So focus on these small steps, one at a time. Each time you complete a step, decide on your next one. Slow and steady. Revisit this exercise whenever you need to.

Part 3: limiting beliefs

'Right, I'm ready to begin,' I hear you cry, 'so, why can't I dive in? What's stopping me?'

I am going to hazard a guess that we've probably all had moments where we've felt the pull to do something new, had a cracking idea that we're excited about, but then something holds us back. What is this? Well, it's very often our own crappy self-doubt that leads to even crappier limiting beliefs forming. For us to take a confident step into the unknown, we're going to need to confront and neutralise any of these first.

To make sense of our lives, we create stories. We take the information that we get, we piece it together and we give it some meaning. That is why two people can have exactly the same experience and yet feel completely different about it.

We like simplicity as humans and often fall foul of something called narrative fallacy. Essentially, this is where we take random events and weave a story together from them, creating logical links or explanations for why something has happened (often ignoring facts or doing some serious mental gymnastics to get there). Author Nassim Taleb popularised our understanding of narrative fallacy in his book *The Black Swan* (2007), in which he describes our human compulsion to create narratives that do not exist, especially when these narratives confirm our already existing beliefs (this is called confirmation bias – when our brains seek out evidence to confirm what we already believe to be true).

The stories we create become the worlds that we live in, so if our stories are full of limiting beliefs – such as the idea we're not good enough or can't do something – then we will build a life based on those ideas rather than creating the life that we want.

In real terms this might look like:

- **The belief:** I believe that anyone who works in the fitness industry is judgemental and mean.
- **Narrative fallacy:** I have pieced this together based on having a PE teacher who was awful to me and my one experience of attending a gym class when the instructor's style was direct and dismissive. Thus my simple story is that everyone who works in fitness is awful.
- **Confirmation bias:** The narrative fallacy means that I then seek out anything that supports my theory and ignore everything else. For example, if I meet a lovely fitness professional then I tell myself that they are an outlier and unusual because they don't fit in with my pre-existing story.
- **Limit on my life:** I don't go to the gym or any fitness classes because I want to avoid people in the fitness industry.

These limiting beliefs are created by our brains to protect us from feeling future pain. It's a pretty clever and simple system, and researchers believe limiting beliefs evolved as a means for us to protect ourselves and survive in this world, such as by encouraging us to avoid danger.

Now, that's all well and good, but as people who want to thrive (not just survive) we have to be mindful of limiting beliefs. If we feel something is holding us back from leaping into the new then it's a good idea to check in on our current beliefs to see if they have any merit or if they are in fact limiting beliefs whittled into the shape of something that looks like fact.

The challenge is that some of our beliefs have been around for a long time, and we may have convinced ourselves that they're insurmountable. They're not. They're thoughts, not physical walls, and we can start to unravel them. To help us understand what limiting beliefs look like I've provided some examples below:

I can't...
'I can't just split up with my partner, what about...'
'I can't just change my career because...'
'I can't do X, Y, Z.'

I don't...
'I don't know where to begin.'
'I don't have the skills to...'
'I don't have any experience, who would even hire me?'

I shouldn't...
'I shouldn't apply for that job because it's rude to my current employer.'
'I shouldn't want to move away, because I know I *should* be grateful for what I have.'
'I shouldn't be thinking like this, because I'm bound to fail anyway.'

I'm not...
'I'm not smart enough.'
'I'm not pretty enough/thin enough/tall enough.'
'I'm not fit enough.'

I've missed the boat...

'I'm too old to start something new.'

'I tried this before but so much time has passed, I'm just too late.'

'Everyone has already started and is way ahead of me.'

They're better...

'My sister is way smarter than me, there's no point in trying.'

'The girl I follow on Instagram is smashing it with her business and I would fail miserably and look stupid if I tried to do something similar.'

'There are so many university graduates coming through now who are way better than me.'

I don't deserve...

'Who am I to want more? I have a roof over my head and that's enough.'

'In the current climate, people are struggling, so why should I have this when others have it so hard?'

'I'm lucky to have a partner who puts up with me and I probably wouldn't find anyone else anyway.'

I was once told...

'My teacher once told me I wasn't creative, so why would I think I can work in design?'

'My dad always told me I had two left feet. I'm not good enough to do a dance class.'

'My mum always told me I give things up, so why would this be any different?'

Do any of the limiting beliefs above sound familiar to you? Take time over the next day or two to notice how you speak to yourself. If you begin to spot limiting beliefs, then you have a choice to make: you can stick with these limiting beliefs that are holding you back or you can call them out and change them. If you'd like to change them, then read on.

Banishing your limiting beliefs

Take your limiting beliefs to court

Let's play a game. I like to call this 'I dispute this, Your Honour'. Jot down some limiting beliefs that you have, then get your pen and paper out because it's time to put your limiting beliefs in front of a jury, one at a time. On your piece of paper, draw a line down the middle and on one side write 'Defence' and on the other write 'Prosecution'. Then it's time to write one of your limiting beliefs at the top of the page.

On the defence side, write down all the reasons this belief is true and the positives for keeping it (e.g. 'If I keep it, I don't have to change or do anything'). On the other side, write all the reasons why your limiting belief is nonsense, and what you lose by allowing it to stay (e.g. 'If I keep it, I'll never have the life I want'). Be honest with yourself and look for evidence that disproves it because, trust me, I know it will be there.

Then at the end of this exercise, you will be the judge and jury, looking at both sides of the argument. It's your job to decide whether you wish to hold on to this limiting belief or lock it up and throw away the key. If it's the slammer for the story then at the bottom of your page I want you to write a better belief that will motivate you to act. For example, 'Learning is part of the process and I embrace it', 'I have all the tools I need to succeed' or 'I am worthy of the life I want.' Repeat this exercise for each limiting belief in turn, as needed.

Allow stories to inspire you

Observing stories of change around us and using them as inspiration is another good way of tackling limiting beliefs. If they can do it, then so can we. Think for a moment whether there's anyone who has tried something new recently and created positive change that you've found inspiring. I bet you can think of someone's rags-to-riches tale you've read about online, or even the empowering story of your cousin's neighbour (the one who left her abusive partner and then fell in love with a kind man in the same year).

For me, the stories of the 'kid from the wrong side of the tracks who sells a great idea to Mark Zuckerberg and becomes an overnight millionaire' feel a little uninspiring. I think it's because they can feel so far removed from my reality that it's hard to imagine how I would do that (even if, factually, I could!).

A story I love is that of my client, Amanda, who wanted a house in the country where she could be 'free to get out in nature' and not feel 'suffocated by the grind of the big city'. Her reality, when we first worked together, was that she had an office job in a city working from 9 a.m. until 6 p.m. Her life was repetitive, busy and with very little time spent outdoors.

Amanda and I looked at all her options together, created a plan (by working through the exercise on pp. 116–21) and then she took action. Within two years, Amanda had upped sticks, quit her job and moved to a rural area where she set herself up as a freelance writer. Amanda had downsized her home and her pay packet but she was the happiest she had ever been. This didn't happen overnight; sacrifices were made and it was brave. There were also a ton of questioning glances from family and friends, but as she walks her springer spaniel across the beautiful English countryside each day, all of that noise pales into insignificance.

Or what about a gorgeous story I read online this week about a guy whose friend called him to say he had broken up with his controlling girlfriend and wanted to meet for a celebratory drink. Our leading man in this story said that at the time he was living a pretty antisocial life so he almost said no to his friend, but something told him to get out of the house that day, so he went along. It turned out that this was to be the night he would meet his now wife. He also shared that when reminiscing about their first meeting, his wife admitted that she too had almost not gone out that evening either.

Stories like this not only melt my soppy heart but they also make me realise just how pivotal these tiny moments of saying yes to new things can be. You see, the more we hear other people's stories and start to believe in the possibility that life can change for us too, the more emboldened we'll feel to ignore anything that's holding us back.

Moment to pause
Before we move on, take some time now to reflect on a few of your favourite inspirational stories of change, so that you can have them to hand the next time you need a little support.

Visualise your success

It's also important to focus on your own personal story of success. To understand that you have the power within you to create new and positive change, regardless of your current circumstances. We can use visualisation as a tool to help support us with this.

Let's begin by picking up on the exercise we did in Part 2 of this chapter. Remind yourself of the area of your life in which you decided to take action – whether that's taking a tap class, starting a new writing project, becoming more adventurous in the kitchen, or whatever else you landed on.

When you have your goal in mind, visualise a time in the future when you have achieved this goal (regardless of how big or small it is) – i.e. you've actioned the change or had the experience that you wanted.

Picture the scene in your mind. Make it as crisp and clear as possible. Where are you? What are you doing? How do you feel?

What does daily life look like? How does this future differ from right now? If taking tap lessons is your goal, then see yourself putting on the tap shoes, walking into the dance studio and hearing the sound of your tap shoes on the floor as you enter the space. See yourself in the mirrored wall among the other dancers in the room, all connected and moving in sync. Have a strong image in your mind and turn up the volume of this movie you're creating. Notice if you can hear, taste, smell or feel anything. Bring your attention to all that you notice around you. Smile to yourself as you breathe in this potential future reality.

Now write this new story out somewhere. Make it compelling. Make this a story you want to be part of, that you want to fight for. Writing things out physically helps cement them in our minds, and a study by Dr Gail Matthews, professor of psychology at Dominican University of California, proved that we're 42 per cent more likely to achieve our goals if we write them down. That sounds like good odds to me, so grab your pen and write down your tale of success. Next time you notice any limiting beliefs floating to the surface, re-read your story for an immediate confidence boost.

Fresh start? I'm ready!

To help you put into practice the techniques we've discussed in this chapter, here are some action points to get you started.

Inside:

1 **From fright to excite.** Work on replacing your fear of the new with excitement of what's to come. Consider why you want to start this new thing and what is exciting about achieving it. List your reasons in your notebook (*see* p. 118 if you need some prompts), and review the list whenever nerves creep in.

2 **Reframe and reclaim.** Reframe your panic sentences that make you worry about the worst-case scenario that could arise from stepping into the new, such as 'If x happens then y happens' (add in something awful that your brain has told you will happen). Rather than saying to yourself, 'If I accept this new job, then I might fail and look stupid', change it to something that helps you reclaim your power, such as, 'If I start this new job and it doesn't work out then I shall look for another job.'

3 **Remember that it's OK if an action doesn't work out as you hoped.** If that happens then you simply try again, tweak what you did, and keep going. You have little to lose and so much to gain. Remind yourself of when you were a child – a time when you didn't overcomplicate trying new things. Instead, you simply ran about kicking a ball, playing hopscotch and, if you fell, you got back up. Be THAT version of yourself when you approach new things in life.

Outside:

1 **Unfold to look bold.** Stepping into new spaces can be daunting. This can manifest as us subconsciously trying to hide, perhaps even folding ourselves into a smaller size. This looks like rolling your shoulders forward, dipping your head and hiding your hands – actions that do not make you look like a confident and interesting person who is ready to connect with their new space. So, check your posture – shoulders back, chin up – and breathe to relax those tense areas of your body. Take up space like you own it.

2 **Try new things.** This is an obvious statement in a chapter about starting something new, but the only way to build confidence in trying new things is ultimately to try new things. Write a list of at least 10 new things that you will try over the next month (perhaps using your brain dump from earlier in Part 2). These could be new foods, new places, meeting new people, trying a new class – whatever they are, just write a list, share it on social media, update your mates on WhatsApp, do whatever works for you. Each new experience is teaching you that you CAN, and with that you're building your 'bank of brave' that will boost your confidence with each deposit.

3 **Sit on a chair, with intention.** This is an actors' exercise based on the Stanislavski principles. Get out a chair and sit on it. The first time you do so, you're simply sitting as you. Notice how you sit and how you feel. Do you fidget or are you still? Now get off the chair and I will give you three different scenarios to have in mind as you sit down again:

i. Sit down as **the confident mum on the school run**. She's the bubbly one who laughs loudly and always seems to be in a lively conversation. Imagine you're her sitting down and waiting for parents' evening to begin. How does she carry herself? What is her posture like? Think about her facial expressions, and her eye contact. I know you likely feel a bit daft doing this exercise but play it out for real. I'm not asking you to do this for an audience.

ii. Sit on the chair as **the CEO of a wildly successful business**. Imagine they are sitting at an awards ceremony getting ready to receive an accolade and have been congratulated on their way in (even hearing a compliment as they take their seat). How would they sit, move, breathe and conduct themselves? Try it out and see how this version differs from 'confident mum'.

iii. Lastly, imagine that you are **a future version of yourself**, who has taken a leap of faith towards something new and made a great choice. You take your seat and get ready to tell someone you love all about the success you have had with a new venture. Consider how this intention changes the posture you initially sat down with at the beginning of this exercise, and how you hold yourself. Do you notice a shift, perhaps a lightness to this version or a swagger that wasn't there earlier?

Enjoy the playfulness of this activity and see how you can bring the confident you of the future (or either of the other two characters) into the next week.

Guest advice

Harriet Thorpe
TV actress (*The Brittas Empire*, *Absolutely Fabulous* and *Eastenders*)
@harriet_thorpe/@hatdorable

"It's always hard starting something new because we are waiting for our supposed critics to come back. I never say to a child be really, really scared and insecure, but subconsciously, habitually one says it to oneself. So, I have to pick up my little self and know that I am going to keep her safe and tell myself that I am enough. This is not about proving myself, it's about being present and enjoying it, because I can choose how I feel and I might as well."

#5

The workplace

I have worn many hats in my lifetime. I've worked in a bank, acted, modelled, worked in coffee shops, been a singer, written books, handed out flyers on the street, been a business owner and worked as a self-development coach, to name but a few. (Plus there was that one time I worked in a seafood restaurant and quit because the old Mexican chef screamed Spanish obscenities at me, and I was fed up of smelling like fish all the time anyway!)

Although some of my jobs have been out of the norm, I understand what it's like to work. I understand that the workplace (whatever your workplace may look like) is a place full to the brim of ways to test your confidence, so it's an important topic to include in this book.

In an ideal world, perhaps you'd prefer to opt out of the workplace completely. To never have to suffer through a 'meeting that should have been an email' again, or never have to make small talk with your colleague whose obsession with Harry Styles is brought up at every single opportunity, every single day (sigh). My friend, I hear you, but unless you have a trust fund or a lottery win stashed under the bed, you're probably going to need to work. So let's get on with feeling as good as we possibly can while we're there.

Before we begin, though, a quick disclaimer. As I've referenced above, my own working life has been rather eclectic, so I want to reassure you that the ideas we'll be discussing here are designed to be transferable. It doesn't matter which rung of the ladder you're currently on or what your working environment may be, the ideas in this chapter have been designed to apply for all. In fact, you might not even be working currently, but this doesn't mean you need to skip this section completely because the information could still be useful (plus we have a whole chapter on the specifics of job interviews in chapter 8).

For example, later on, I'll talk us through asking for a pay rise. The same 'difficult conversation' template used here could also be applied when approaching a difficult conversation with a family member or friend. Or you might even find yourself joining the workforce again in the future, in which case, with this information, you'll be all set.

Common confidence challenges in the workplace

I recently asked my followers on social media to submit the biggest confidence challenges they have faced at work. When the answers came in, it was fascinating to see that so many of the answers – across age and gender – outlined the same scenarios time and time again.

I also have to be honest here and admit that I did receive some hilarious embarrassing moment stories too. My top awkward moment was shared by someone who had spent 10 minutes being highly critical of the new team leader (with a shameful amount of ruthless detail), to then become suddenly and uncomfortably aware that the team leader was in fact the mother of the person they were talking to. Ouch.

In terms of scenarios where people feel unconfident in the workplace, I've compiled a list of the most popular situations overleaf. And although everyone's personal experience of these situations may be unique to them, the same thread ran through every single response: the worry of not being good enough, failing, and saying or doing the wrong thing. Let's take a look at these situations, in no particular order:

- Asking for a pay rise or promotion.
- Speaking up in meetings.
- Doing presentations (which is covered in chapter 1).
- Not feeling good enough.
- Standing up for yourself (which we have a whole section on in chapter 3).
- Fear of failure.
- Perfectionism, e.g. setting very high standards for yourself and not meeting them.
- Staff room conversations and fostering good working relationships with colleagues (check out chapter 2 for help with this).

Sound familiar?

None of us like the feeling that we might 'get it wrong' in front of our peers. As a result, we can find ourselves playing out some pretty far-fetched examples in our minds of what might happen should we dare to raise our heads above the parapet and try to succeed. It's human to feel like this though, and there isn't a person out there who doesn't experience this in their lifetime (even the ones who look like they don't – I promise you they do!).

Essentially, we're all scared to fail and we're scared that failure will mean we aren't enough. In the workplace, this can feel particularly heightened as our continued success at work is linked to money coming in to support ourselves and our family. There is also the social aspect of work to contend with (work nights out, chit-chat in the office) and various hierarchies to navigate too. Essentially, there's a lot going on! So, if finding your confidence in the workplace is a challenge for you, then please know you're not alone, and there are lots of techniques we can try to give you the support you need.

Fear of failure

Fear of failure is often the underlying reason for so many of our decisions. It feels awful to mess up, it stings like hell to fail and our brains are wired to avoid it at all costs. Our brains hate failure so much because failure equals uncertainty, and the potential that others might not see us as valuable. If we're not seen as valuable then we might be left out of the group (see p. 37 for more on group safety). Experiencing a sense of isolation from the group can activate the brain's survival instincts, leading to an exaggerated perception of the stakes involved, often making situations appear more risky than they truly are.

Why is this? Well, the brain deduces that failure = 'pushed out' = 'left out' = 'on my own' = 'dead in a ditch'. I'm oversimplifying here, of course, but our brains are historically wired for survival, so they assume the worst in order to be ready to protect us. Hence why doing a work presentation can feel so risky: the subtext in our brains is that if we mess up then we'll be pushed out of the group and be ... yep, you've got this ... dead in a ditch.

I must stress that none of this is conscious; it's all very much hidden under the surface. I don't remember having ever stepped up to do something that scared me and consciously thinking that if I failed, I would literally die (however, I do remember having feelings of this intensity!).

The brain's tendency to switch to survival mode can often have us finding dangers where there are none. So, if left unchecked, you could be scared off taking a leap of faith or stepping out of your comfort zone at work. This will have you not putting yourself forward for that new role, swerving the chance to lead a meeting or avoiding doing that training conference, all because of the noisy 'what ifs?' running through your head.

Last year, a client shared that five times she had wanted to put herself forward for a promotion, but she'd held back each time. She was worried that if she were unsuccessful then her colleagues would see her as a failure. Five times she had wanted to give it a shot but had not, and five times she had watched less experienced people than her walk into the more senior positions that she could do standing on her head.

Failure also brings up embarrassment and a huge dollop of shame. We sadly shame ourselves *a lot* about *a lot* of things, but it does *not* do a lot to change anything. Yet we shame ourselves when we fail in some misguided attempt to make ourselves do better next time. This doesn't work. Shaming ourselves doesn't produce positive outcomes; instead, it keeps us stuck. We become inactive, terrified of failing and shaming ourselves again, and then fed up that we're not doing or achieving the things we want. Knowing all of this, is it any wonder that so many of us choose to avoid situations in which we could potentially fail?

But being confident is very closely linked to our attitude to failure. It is about trusting ourselves enough that when we fail (which we inevitably will, time and time again), then we'll get straight back up and work it out. People with high levels of self-belief aren't afraid to fail because they recognise that it is simply part of the process; it's no reflection on them personally, it's simply how we learn and progress. Failing just means we're one step closer to the next success. So, the quicker we embrace failure, get comfortable with the uncomfortable, and trust our ability to bounce back after a fall, then the quicker we'll see ourselves thriving and flourishing in confidence in the workplace.

"The quicker we embrace failure and **trust our ability to bounce back** after a fall, then the quicker we'll see ourselves **thriving** and **flourishing in confidence** in the workplace."

Moment to pause

Before we move on, take a few minutes to breathe. Then let's repeat this affirmation to ourselves (out loud if you can, but in your mind or written down if not): 'I am not a failure. The project might have failed, the idea might have failed, I may have failed to get the job, but the failures say *nothing* about my character.'

Now I think it's time to dig into the specifics of workplace challenges. For the rest of the chapter, we'll focus on three scenarios from our original list on p. 134. We're going to deep-dive into:

1. how to speak up in meetings;

2. how to ask for a pay rise;

3. how to start believing that you're good enough.

I've selected these three topics because they're challenges that come up repeatedly with my clients and in my wider Happy Me Project community. Also, I think much of what we learn through these three scenarios can be applied to the majority of workplace situations we find ourselves in. So, even if these specific scenarios aren't relevant to you right now, I suggest you read them anyway and see what tips you can find for your personal workplace woes.

Scenario 1: how to speak up in meetings

You're sitting in a beige meeting room on a black leather office chair (that for some reason is squeaking every time you move). There are 10 people crammed around a boardroom table that's littered with jugs of water and cups of now-cold coffee. It's warmer than anyone would like in there and the light is making a buzzing sound as

'Corporate Kevin' is delivering another long-winded word dump that doesn't seem to mean anything or go anywhere.

You have a point to make. You've internally rolled your eyes a thousand times and actively disagreed with more than one person, only it's all been in your head. The idea of actively voicing your opinion to the nine other people in the room fills you with dread, and so you just sit there, hoping that at some point this afternoon someone other than Kevin will say something. You are not alone.

I work with men and women around the world who have shared similar stories of their own frustration and desire to have the confidence to use their voice in meetings. So why don't they just speak up and shut Corporate Kevin down?

Well, some of my clients tell me it's because they fear that what they say might not be good enough, and people will judge them, or else they'll reveal themselves as incompetent. Others worry about knowing when is an appropriate time to jump in, and others dread the moment before they speak when the room becomes silent and everyone turns to look at them. Or often clients tell me that they want to hold back their ideas until they're perfect. Also, if you've not spoken up before and have been the habitual quiet one, the worry is that it'll be a huge deal when you finally do speak, which can feel like an incredible amount of pressure on your shoulders.

Whatever the reason, there is nothing worse than waiting to make a point, only to have 'Won't Stop Talking Ruth' say the exact thing you had been thinking all along and taking all the credit. Shall we work out how you can start speaking up then? I feel like we should.

Before the meeting

Reframe the 'why'
If your mind is fixed on the reason for speaking up as being to show you know what you're talking about, to flex your expertise or to add

some incredibly insightful value the moment you open your mouth, then you might find that the pressure is all a little too much.

How about we reframe the reason for speaking up as 'I'm going to share some thoughts and ask questions in order to help the team. My contribution could potentially unlock a thought from someone else, so that together we can help move the discussion along.'

Framing the idea of you speaking up as a helpful part of the process so that you, as a team, can find the solutions together, is a way more helpful – and less stressful! – approach than seeing speaking up in a meeting as an opportunity to seek individual glory.

There are also those of you who worry that if you aren't agreeable in a meeting, you will appear negative or that you're not being a team player. I'm going to hand this over to Reed Hastings, the CEO of Netflix, who shared his approach to this mentality. He believes that to 'disagree silently is disloyal to Netflix'. That is, if you disagree with something but choose not to voice it, you're choosing not to help. Ouch, well that gets us right in the gut (especially the people pleasers of us in the bunch). So that's the reframe. It's not negative to share ways things can be done better, it's helpful. A teeny tiny caveat here: when you are disagreeing with whatever is currently happening, it's useful (where appropriate) to offer an alternative solution, too.

At this point, it's also, once again, essential for us to know *why* it's important for us to speak up. I can give you all the tools about the ways you can deliver and prepare, but if you don't have any motivation to speak then you won't.

What would speaking up offer you? Would it mean you'll be seen as an engaged team player who might be given more exciting opportunities? Would speaking up about a special interest of yours mean you could become the go-to person for that topic? Would you improve your company visibility, giving people outside of your immediate team the opportunity to get to know how great you are?

Then let's go a step further and ask ourselves why we want any of that stuff. If we were offered more opportunities, the chance to develop a specialism or a heightened company visibility, what would we gain? A sense of purpose or to feel some accomplishment? Perhaps it could even mean more money or another step towards a bigger goal that you have? Thinking about the motivation behind speaking up can be the propellent to encourage you to take action.

> **Moment to pause**
> Now would be a great time to reflect on the prompts above and ask yourself what's your *why* for speaking up? Take the time you need before moving on.

Prepare and practise

Can you prepare things in advance, so that you have notes ready with some questions and talking points? Some of these talking points will be work-related but don't be scared to think of some general chit-chat ideas too. I know not everyone needs this, but some of us do and there's nothing wrong with that. Ideas might be: the weather, a recent big event or a comment about the building you're in. (For more support with this, see p. 55). Practise saying your comments out loud before the meeting, and if you have someone to practise with then even better – or if not, practising to your cat is fine too.)

Warm up

Just like an athlete preparing for a big game, we can prepare for speaking up by stretching our mouths and warming up our voices. For a bit of fun, try some vocal warm-ups on Spotify or YouTube to get you ready; simply search 'quick vocal warm up' for some helpful ideas. Or at the very least, I suggest you spend time opening your mouth as wide as you can, then pretending to chew bubble gum while humming (maybe do this at home to avoid strange looks!). I know this might seem 'silly', but you're sending signals to your brain that you're about to speak up and this will serve you well in the moment.

Find your allies

Now I (of course) want you to feel super empowered and brave as you share your ideas, whatever the situation. However, I also appreciate, as you are growing this speaking-up muscle, that you might find it helpful to have a buffer. This can come in the form of work colleague allies.

A good friend of mine, Kirsty, shared that when she first started out in the workplace (and was a little wet around the ears), she would often speak to someone more senior prior to a meeting. In these more intimate, one-to-one conversations, she was able to get feedback before sharing her ideas in the more intimidating group setting. This would help Kirsty feel more confident in the meeting itself, and it'd often mean that the senior person would call on Kirsty to share her ideas at an appropriate point. It made her feel a little braver to know she already had someone onside.

Consider too that a part of being confident is about sharing, vulnerably, the times when you're not feeling so self-assured. This may look like telling your manager that you can feel a little nervous in a group setting. This doesn't mean that you then don't have to speak, but it means you have the confidence that someone else, other than you, is aware that this is a skill you're still working on.

This isn't weak, this doesn't look inept; it looks like a damn brave human who is sharing that even though they find something a challenge, they're still going to give it a go. We are allowed to be nuanced humans who can be fabulous at their jobs while also finding some areas hard. Two truths can coexist, so find those allies.

The meeting is here

Say something – ripping the bandage off

The meeting has begun, and the key here is to hit the ground running and get started early. Rip the bandage off and say something as soon as you walk into the room (online or physical). What you say doesn't have to be momentous. (Remember: you've prepared those talking points beforehand, so pick one of them, for example: 'The weather is glorious today' or 'Did you do anything nice at the weekend?') The quicker you have said something, the better you will feel, so put your game face on and let's go!

Set yourself a target

Having a target for how often you want to speak during the meeting can be helpful. Joel Garfinkle, an executive leadership coach, suggests speaking at least three times. One time could be a comment you have prepared in advance (perhaps something about the weather or one of our other small-talk examples, see p. 55 for more); the second could be a pre-prepared question or comment; and the third could be something that comes to your mind during the meeting itself. (Remember: this can be a simple question or comment – it does not have to be the best idea or comment you've ever come up with.)

Body language

An important factor in how we come across to others in our daily lives is our body language, and in meetings (either in-person or online), it's no different. Basic body language to help you appear confident includes: sitting or standing up straight or leaning in, maintaining some eye contact* and facing the person who is talking.

----

* My neurodivergent comrades, I appreciate that eye contact can be challenging for some of us; I have ADHD and my constant need to wriggle and move is also something I often need to keep in check. As with all differences between neurotypical and neuro-spicy folks, we can understand ourselves, explain ourselves (if appropriate and when needed), and ask for understanding from others when something is just too much for us. But we can also experiment with some of this body language stuff too and see if any of it gives us a better outcome. So, do what you can and don't judge what you can't. This is about the full picture here, not just one component.

In terms of online meetings, make sure you adjust your camera to the right height (no one wants to see up your nose), look directly into the camera when speaking (to give the impression of eye contact), and sit up straight with no secret scrolling while someone else is talking. If you're a fidget (like me), be mindful that this can look a lot bigger on screen, so find other ways to move, such as using (silent) fidget toys off screen or wiggling your toes.

Ultimately, most body language rules apply across the board: smile, sit up straight and nod in agreement where appropriate. You've got this.

In 2012, the world was wowed by Harvard psychologist Amy Cuddy's TED Talk on 'power posing'. Cuddy's research showed that if we stand or sit in dominant positions then it can impact not only how we are perceived, but also how powerful we feel internally too (and these effects can be felt after only a minute of posing). Some of these poses include the 'Superman pose' (standing up straight, hands on your hips), the 'CEO pose' (sitting down, hands behind your head) and the 'high V' pose (arms above your head in a V-shape). Since then, the research has become a little blurry as to whether people actually *feel* different after adopting these poses, but there's no doubt they certainly help people *look* more powerful. Try them out and see if they affect how you are perceived in the workplace, and if you feel more powerful as a result, then that's a bonus!

Hilariously, back in 2015, it appears that the UK Conservative party had been given some of Cuddy's research, because they all began adopting a (very!) wide leg stance in a clear attempt to look more powerful. Sadly their power posing was more than a little over the top and instead of looking authoritative it ended up looking ... well ... really odd (take a look for yourself by googling 'Tory power pose' and have a giggle!).

Hands

We want to see your hands and, more specifically, we want to see your thumbs. Sounds odd, right? I'm aware I've probably conjured up images of a dorky human holding their thumbs up at their boss while bemused colleagues look on. So, I'll explain…

Our brains are programmed to spend a lot of time keeping an eye on people's hands. This stems back to Neanderthal times when we were potentially carrying weapons and so our hands (and our thumbs in particular since we need them to hold these weapons) were dangerous. Even though we would hope that you don't have to be on the lookout for weapons in the hands of Debra from marketing, your brain trusts Debra more if you can see her hands (and her thumbs).

We are also programmed to see those who talk with their hands as more confident. You only have to catch a glimpse of a politician, comedian or presenter on screen to see that they all use a high level of gesticulation, and look damn confident doing so.

In real terms then, during your meeting, keep your hands visible – on the table or on your lap (if there is no table) – and make sure we can also see those thumbs! Talk using your hands and, for those who don't find this natural, take time to practise beforehand. It might feel odd at first but it'll have a huge impact on how you come across. Give it a try.

Keep track

During the meeting, be sure to listen and take notes so you can record any questions or new ideas you might have as the meeting progresses. Taking notes is going to help you feel confident that you're staying abreast of everything that is going on. Also, when you do speak, these notes can help support you if you feel anxious, since they can act as your own little cheat sheet to remind you of your brilliant ideas.

Personally, I take a ton of notes during meetings because my bouncy ADHD brain is firing off all the time. This means that if I don't write it down, I will definitely forget what I was going to say. Try note-taking in your next meeting and, if it works for you, add it to your confidence-boosting toolkit.

Post-meeting (next steps)

The meeting is done. You say your goodbyes. You head back to your desk to breathe a sigh of relief. If it's an online meeting then you close your laptop screen (after doing the obligatory awkward goodbye wave and forced smile) and enjoy a moment of stillness. You did it! You survived. Now it's time to take stock and set some intentions for next time.

Did you manage to say anything?

If so, be proud of yourself. Even if this time you stuttered and stumbled over your words, congratulate yourself. You managed to get *something* vaguely coherent out – you did it and we work from here. Once you have sufficiently praised your lovely self (and do not skip this step please because it's an extremely important part of the process), we can move on to considering where we can grow from here and setting intentions for our next meeting. This might look like writing a list of what went well, reflecting on the techniques you tried – those that weren't for you and those you definitely want to remember to use again.

If you didn't manage to say anything (yet!)

If you didn't quite manage to speak up this time, does this mean that you should give yourself a hard time and throw in the towel? Absolutely not. Not on my watch!

You are a work in progress – we all are. Remind yourself that not achieving a desired outcome immediately is part of the process. When we don't achieve something, we go again. I also have an exercise for you to try.

Get a pen and paper out. Draw a line down the middle and on one side write 'My wins' and on the other side write 'Things to tweak'. Fill out ideas on both sides and remember to be kind to yourself. Think of your wins first. Even if you didn't speak, perhaps you noticed that you felt a tad more confident than normal? Were your hands displayed on the table or did you take some good notes during the meeting? Then turn to your tweaks. Perhaps next time you'll try having a chat with a colleague before the meeting about your ideas, or maybe confiding in your boss that you find the meetings intimidating? Or maybe you'll make more notes before the meeting next time? The habit of staying quiet may take a little unsticking and that's OK. Be gentle with yourself as you go.

Scenario 2: how to ask for a pay rise

You've been in your job for a while, you've been doing pretty damn fabulous work, you notice things are going well for the company, and perhaps you've seen others reaping the rewards. This may then prompt you to consider that you should ask for a pay rise.

The thought of asking for more money, for many people, can make them feel squeamish. You might feel worried you will come across as too pushy or unworthy of more money. Or the mere thought of having this encounter with a superior may trigger serious imposter syndrome (defined as a person's inability to believe their success is deserved and legitimately achieved). Many people would rather avoid the difficult conversation about pay altogether for fear of their boss saying no.

BUT I want you to be paid handsomely for your time. I want you to have a great life and have the money to support this. I'm pretty sure that you would like these things for yourself, too, so I'm going to help you get out of your own way and ask for more.

Before the meeting

Do your research
The first step on deciding to ask for a pay rise is to gather knowledge. What are other people in similar roles to you being paid in your industry? If you're unsure about what people are earning then check

out the website Glassdoor. Know what you want, get a number in your head and get ready to ask for it.

As someone who currently works for myself, I have often had to feel my way through the question of 'How much should I charge?' I remember the first time I increased my 1:1 coaching price and someone actually paid that new price. I remember it because I panicked so severely that I launched my phone across the room (I do this now and then when I need a moment to process what's on the phone and, yes, I have cracked it on occasion and, no, I do not recommend it). I share this because I know what it's like to feel nervy about this stuff and it's OK if you feel uncomfortable too (just maybe try not to throw things!).

Prep your achievements

Note what you have done for your company in the last year, including any responsibilities and achievements. Grab your notebook and write it all down. This is not a time to be humble and if you find yourself slipping into a 'humble mumble', then try imagining you were putting this together for a friend. If this were a list for someone you cared about, what would be on it?

Script

You might even want to get your actor on and write a script. I would actively encourage this. Now, don't freak out, I'm not asking you to put together a flash mob-style pay-rise dance, but writing down a template of what you would like to get across is a very helpful tool. Practise this script out loud with your shoulders back, chin up and an open posture.

Notify your manager

Book a time to speak with your manager and give them a prior understanding of what the topic of the meeting will be. This gives them time to prepare, too, and will mean everyone feels confident about their role.

Clothing

On the day of the meeting, you want to feel your most comfortable self, so dress to impress but in a way that feels good to you. Don't fall into the trap of dressing in some performative nonsense for how you think you 'should' look. If you're uncomfortable in your clothing then that's not going to make you feel great in the meeting.

Anxiety tools

If you're feeling anxiety creep in (and, let's be honest, it's highly likely that you are), implement some anxiety-busting techniques before the meeting. This might be calm breathing (*see* p. 24 for some different techniques), meditation, listening to music, dancing, going for a walk or any other tools you have found beneficial before (I have popped some more anxiety-busting tools at the end of this chapter too). Don't be hard on yourself if your anxiety level is high. Before any stage show I have ever performed in, I have been so full of adrenaline and nervous energy that I have had to do press-ups and run on the spot before going on stage, to get it out of my system. It's normal.

The meeting is here

Rapport

Walk into the meeting with a smile and human-to-human chat. Find some common ground and use it to spark a conversation (weather, the time of year, the space you're in) and just be your lovely self. We are far more likely to give people things when we like them and connect with them, so don't hide who you are.

I once spoke to a very important theatre director in London, who told me that if two people auditioned for him and one was good and pleasant, and the other was exceptional but rude, he would hire the good actor every time. The director said he didn't want to work with someone he didn't like, so he'd rather help the good actor become exceptional. This is a handy thing to remember when you're feeling pressure to be perfect.

Straight facts and evidence

Set out clearly what you want. This might be the area of the meeting you have scripted and rehearsed (don't be scared to do either of these things). For example: 'Thank you for having this meeting with me. I have enjoyed working for the company over the last few years and being able to play a part in our success. I am excited about where we are headed and have lots of ideas about how I can help with that growth, so I would like to discuss the opportunity to increase my pay.'

Then supply your evidence. This is where you can use those facts you found and popped in your fancy notebook. You can share that the industry standard is X, Y, Z and list the ways in which you have brought business in, the responsibilities you take on, and any of those juicy achievements.

Language

A little note on delivery and language while discussing the straight facts and evidence: be mindful of avoiding apologetic language. For example, avoid phrases such as 'Does that make sense?' or 'I hope this is OK?' We think we are softening the blow by presenting the information in this way, but all we're actually doing is using our own doubt to plant niggles of doubt in our manager's mind too.

Instead, if we say things directly, in a matter-of-fact way, without a question mark at the end, then the confidence we show will make our manager feel more confident in our request. Why wouldn't they, when you're sitting there, the epitome of poise and certitude?

Also be mindful not to slip into anecdotal reasons why you would like the pay rise. I mean *we* know you want to use the money to do up your kitchen and finally set a date for your wedding, but your boss doesn't need to hear this bit. They want to hear how their spend will mean the company thrives and flourishes, so keep it straight to the point. (And then you can share with me your exciting plans for your pay rise instead – send them over to me on Instagram @iamhollymatthews – because I'd love to hear!)

Post-meeting (next steps)

You've pleaded your case and the meeting is almost over. The chances are that your manager will now need some time before giving you an answer, since it likely won't be their decision alone to make. It's a good time, therefore, to ask about timelines, for example when the decision will be made and when you should expect to hear back from them.

Perhaps, however, you've got a definitive answer. If the answer is a yes, it's time to thank your manager and head straight off to do a jubilant dance somewhere private (air punching and whooping are also nice alternatives).

If it's a no, then ask for a reason why, or for constructive feedback on your performance (I know, I know, this bit makes us want to vomit, but remember that confident people aren't afraid of this because it creates an opportunity to be better). Feedback on your performance will allow you to ask for the opportunity to hit any targets they have set for you and revisit this conversation in six or 12 months' time (whatever feels appropriate). However, a no may have nothing to do with your performance and everything to do with company policy and performance overall. If that's the case, then again, ask to revisit the discussion and stick a reminder for yourself in your calendar.

Regardless of the outcome – positive, negative or inconclusive – you need to take a moment to recognise that you have just completed a nerve-wracking conversation and therefore had a MASSIVE win. You did it! Plus the worst-case scenario didn't materialise (you didn't die and your manager didn't tell you to leave and never darken their doorway again – or enter your own worst-case scenario, as appropriate!). So, what's next? Well, you do it again, at a later date, and feel even more confident the second time round because you know you can do it now.

Scenario 3: how to start believing that you're good enough

Working as a self-development coach, I get a huge amount of feedback and messages from readers, clients and followers on social media. This allows me to have a real collective look at us as human beings. The one thing I can tell you without a shadow of a doubt is this: everyone you know, and every human out there, at some point thinks they aren't good enough.

Now this isn't said to minimise your feelings but to let you know that this quirk of humanity is not unique to you. Instead, it's a symptom of how we live and the pressures we put on ourselves. And do you want to know the uncomfortable truth?

We aren't enough... We aren't enough to live up to the impossible expectations we place upon ourselves.

For those of you who have these 'I'm not good enough' feelings, I am fairly sure they sit side by side with their ugly cousin, perfectionism. Perfectionism is where we refuse to accept anything short of the impossibly perfect standards that we have set for ourselves. This can often leave us stuck where we are because we're too afraid to try. We're afraid to try because we *know* we will definitely fall short of the exaggerated expectations we've put on ourselves. And when we do try, often we'll end up running ourselves into the ground as we try to reach our excruciatingly high bar.

The power of acceptance

So how do we lift our self-esteem and lower our feelings of inadequacy? We start with acceptance. I know we want a magic 'I will be confident at work' super-pill. However, understanding where we might have dips in our confidence, and owning this, can be the key to unlocking what's going on, and raising our self-esteem in the process.

It's a weird paradox that if we accept that we might always have to support ourselves (by using techniques to calm our nerves, enlisting the support of work allies or doing a fair bit of pre-work before our meetings), then this acceptance of perceived weaknesses might actually find us feeling more confident in taking steps forward at work.

Accepting that you find time management difficult, for example, may mean that you feel confident to seek support with this, thus allowing you to feel more confident you won't be late or take too long with something. Accepting that you are always going to have to make a conscious effort to be more vocal at work, and that this doesn't come naturally to you, can have the impact of taking the pressure off you trying to be like your chattier colleagues. It allows you to create a scaffold of support when you know it's time to speak up.

Since my diagnosis of ADHD, I've stopped feeling 'less than' about certain aspects of my personality that were related to this, such as time blindness and impulsivity. I used to find myself constantly apologising for being too early, for example, but I was early to avoid the constant anxiety about being late. I stopped being so hard on myself for getting excited in the moment and impulsively agreeing to something, even if later I went away and found it wasn't possible to do. My acceptance of these traits has allowed me to speak up, advocate for myself, ask for help when needed and feel way more confident in these areas by default.

Avoiding negative external messaging

While working on personal acceptance, we must also keep an eye on where we might be getting external messaging that we aren't good enough. Be mindful of receiving unhelpful external commentary that we need to *do* or *be* more.

A quick gander at any blog, magazine or social media site will tell us that we need to be many contradictory things at once, while juggling an inordinate number of balls, to be seen as successful. Once you notice what is feeding you the lie that you're not completely fabulous as you are, then you can start to look at tweaks you can make to change this.

For example, maybe you have been watching some gorgeous single woman's social media feed. She is running her own business, jetting around the globe, making lots of money and living a vibrant and independent lifestyle that you find yourself drooling over.

You then compare your own world, even though your circumstances are very different. Instead, you're over here desperately juggling a new baby and childcare with emails and trying to get to work on time. You are most certainly not going to fancy-pants business meetings on a Maui beach. I mean, you'd just be happy to do your emails while not smelling like baby vomit and nappy rash cream.

The tweak here could be as simple as unfollowing said gorgeous, independent businesswoman, so you can stop beating yourself with a tidal wave of comparison. Or perhaps you learn to focus on aspects of her lifestyle that you like (for example, she appears to be her own boss, which is appealing to you) but you recognise that your route to this may be a little different, and that's fine.

According to my social media feed today: I should have a degree but then also I don't need one because all the successful entrepreneurs are college drop-outs anyway. I need to have a six-figure salary but also I need to not be *too* ambitious because family should be my focus. I should also give everything to my business but then go with the flow, not burn out and practise lots of self-care, too.

The conflicting messaging can leave us turning on ourselves and assuming we just aren't good enough. When, in fact, we are. The problem is not us but the completely unobtainable goals we're told to achieve, which are impossible for anyone other than a few outliers (or for those who choose to tell big untruths on social media).

If anything, this knowledge can be incredibly relieving. We can use it to empower ourselves to find our own way to work success, and even use it as a catalyst to define what 'work success' means and looks like for us as the individual people that we are. Be mindful of what and who you are letting into your world and remind yourself daily that even the people you think have it all figured out, don't. Everyone is perfectly imperfect and that's how it will always be.

From awkward in the staffroom to badass in the boardroom

To help you put into practice the techniques we've discussed in this chapter, here are some action points to get you started.

Inside:

1 **Write down** why you want to do well at work. At the top of the page write: 'I want to succeed at work because... [and add in your answer].' Then further down on the page, write: 'Doing great at work will allow me to... [and again, pop in your answer].' Take a picture of this and save it on your phone. Before entering a situation where you need to 'show up' and it feels hard, look at this to remind yourself of your motivation.

2 **Calm that anxiety** by stimulating your vagus nerve (the longest nerve in your body that is responsible for calming your organs down after a period of fight or flight). By stimulating the vagus nerve, you can send a message to your body that it's time to relax and destress, which can be incredibly helpful when entering potentially stressful work situations. Do this by:

- humming or singing;
- chewing gum;
- self-massage (a gentle shoulder and neck rub for two minutes);
- gently pulling and rubbing your ears;
- splashing cold water on your face;

- belly breathing – this means taking nice full breaths in and really pushing out and filling your diaphragm and belly area as you do so, then slowly breathing out.

3 Visualise a positive outcome – this is simply imagining (like you might have done as a child) and it can be wonderful at nudging your brain towards your desired outcome. Before going into a meeting, take time the night before to imagine yourself doing brilliantly. Visualise your body posture and hear yourself speaking confidently. Imagine the other people being friendly and engaging with you. Notice how you feel in this imagined moment and breathe in this version of your life.

Outside:

1 Practise talking with your hands. Go way over the top at first by wandering around your home chatting to yourself out loud and making huge hand and arm gestures as you go. Practise this both sitting and standing. For some of you, even the slightest hand gesture will feel huge, so going over the top like this initially will help stretch your comfort zone.

I worked with an Italian business leader once who confidently told me he didn't need to work on this because 'all Italian people speak with their hands with ease'. After watching him use the tiniest, tamest hand gestures known to man (and then showing him this by filming his performance), we both recognised there was work to be done. If you're trying to influence in a meeting or interview, how it *looks*, not how it feels, matters most, so try recording yourself or look in a mirror as you practise.

2 Notice how nerves show up for you in your body language. Perhaps you play with your wedding ring or rub your neck. Maybe you're a nail or cheek biter. Knowing what you do when you're nervous can be the first step in minimising this behaviour. You might need to ask someone close to you what you do, since you may not even be aware of some of your tells. This doesn't matter in your social life or when you're not trying to make an impact, but at work when you want to influence or look your most confident self, it can help to be aware of these signs and rein them in.

3 Look like a winner. We, as humans, have to make snap decisions and in the workplace this can be extremely prevalent. Does this person look like a winner or not? Ruthless, I know. Winners take up space; they own a room and their body language reflects this. Practise taking up space by standing tall, straightening your back, rolling your shoulders back, putting your chin up and planting your feet firmly on the ground. Be mindful of low-power postures and avoid them, such as crossing your arms across your body or having your shoulders rolling forwards or raised up to your ears.

Guest advice

Samantha Harman
Style coach
@thestyleeditor

❝When your outfit feels like YOU on your best day, you can forget about it and focus on bringing all your skills and expertise to your work. Your wardrobe should be your best employee; it should be working FOR you, not you always feeling like you have to change or shrink or hide parts of yourself. Style works best when you lean into your magic, not always trying to fight against it with someone else's outdated idea of what a [insert job title] should look like. Dress to celebrate yourself and you will bring so much more joy and confidence into your working life.❞

#6

Relationships

I'd like to begin by telling you a story. Growing up, I had a friend called … let's call her 'Katy' (for the sake of anonymity). Katy was a master at morphing herself into whatever she felt other people needed her to be. Over the years, she changed dramatically as her relationships came and went.

Now, of course it's pretty normal to change and even to lean into new things while in a relationship, but Katy's changes were extreme and always in alignment with whomever she was spending the most time with. She'd change many aspects of herself, such as her look, opinions, likes, dislikes and even sometimes her accent, based on the relationship that she was in.

At one point she was heavily into football while dating Darren (his name actually *is* Darren or Daz but I feel like there are so many Darrens who like football that we're gonna be OK on this one). Darren was a man I can only describe as an old-school football hooligan (think skinhead and the film *The Football Factory*). Katy started supporting his local football team and began trekking around the UK to their away games. She'd never been to a football game before she met him and the intensity of the shift was noticeable.

The following year Daz was gone and so was the football. Instead, Katy was going out with a tattooed gothic guy from Wales called Mark, who kept ferrets and once told me that one of them was the reincarnation of his late mum. Suddenly, Katy had 20 piercings, a tattoo sleeve, and was living with the guy, his ferrets and his late mum (in ferret form).

We lost touch over the years but the last time I saw Katy she was married to a posh city banker in London. The piercings were gone, the tattoo sleeve was covered, and she was telling me about a 'simply thrilling' night they'd had at the Savile Club (an elite London Members club). She was sporting a plummy English accent that was rather alien to her working-class northern roots, and there wasn't a football shirt or ferret in sight.

I really hope Katy is doing well and I certainly believe that we (and 'Katy') can be whoever we wish to be. We can change our minds, we can change our look and, if we wish, we can change our accents. The reason I use Katy as an example though is that her motivation for change has seemingly always been to attract and impress the partner whom she is with at the time. As a person on the sidelines of her life, I noticed her giving away her agency by following and doing things that the other person liked, while potentially abandoning her own beliefs, wants and needs. As a British person I would often 'poke fun' or 'take the piss' (as we say here) at her behaviour, but ultimately, I never felt it my place to raise it any further.

How losing yourself in a relationship can cause low self-esteem

I have my own story of losing myself to a relationship, too. I met my first boyfriend at just 17 and during my years in this relationship I lost a lot of who I was. We were very different people from the start, with different aspirations, backgrounds and world views, although as teenagers we can be forgiven for overlooking all that stuff, as we just wanted to have fun with someone we found attractive. But over time, my boyfriend's expectations of how I should behave or what I should wear meant I started to feel pressure to change myself to fit his needs … while neglecting my own.

Year after year, I gave away my power by changing myself slowly but surely to fulfil his needs. I dressed in a way that he preferred and acted a certain way when we socialised together to please him. I convinced myself that the choices I was making were my own, but every time I chose to accept my boyfriend's preferences over my own, my confidence was chipped away at. It was sneaky. I slowly lost my sense of self and didn't notice what I was allowing to happen. Those around me tried their best to flag this to me, but I was blinded by wanting the relationship to work. But it didn't.

The reason for this was that my boyfriend was in love with a carefully curated character whom I had sculpted to be exactly what he needed. It wasn't working because I wasn't being true to myself. It wasn't working because I wasn't feeling seen, heard or valued by my partner – all the important requirements needed in any fulfilling and secure relationship. Instead, I was suffering the pain and low self-esteem of never feeling good enough as myself, constantly modifying to try to please him.

'Confidence and self-esteem come from **understanding who you are** and **embracing this completely**.'

In our quest to be loved, we can sometimes foolishly believe that the more we can become like that other person, then the more chance we will have of being loved. Instead, we actually create a barrier between ourselves and our partners as we start to feel like they don't know us at all (because they likely don't). Then when the relationship ends, we're left questioning who we are.

Let's take a look at how a lack of self-confidence may begin to present itself in the reality of our day-to-day relationships because, spoiler alert, it can be pretty damn destructive! Low self-esteem in relationships can begin to show up as – take a big breath in here! – neediness, being clingy, being oversensitive, jealously, people-pleasing behaviour, enabling bad behaviours from your partner, cheating, lying, snooping, having unrealistic expectations of your relationship, fear of decision-making, asking your partner for permission to do things … and the list really does go on and on (you can breathe again now).

Maybe you're currently in a relationship where you don't feel as confident as you should. If so, then please don't worry my dear friend because you aren't alone and wherever you are right now is absolutely not the place you need to stay. Let's look at how to feel strong and confident and create relationships that fill you with joy. A little note to remind you that these don't have to just be romantic relationships. And even if you're not in a romantic relationship now, you may be in the future, so use the transferable lessons in this chapter regardless of where you're at.

The importance of getting to know yourself

You see, you don't need to change who you are to find love or a great relationship. But you do need to know yourself well enough first, so you can then be *yourself* to its fullest extent and, by doing so, attract the right person into your world. The more connected you are with yourself, the more connected you can be with others because when you show people who you truly are, and if they like it, that is a connection like no other. Confidence and self-esteem come from understanding who you are and embracing this completely.

Taking stock – an exercise

Take a moment to consider the relationships you have in your world right now and *who* you are in those relationships. I want you to notice if you feel you are able to be your truest self. It's fine to adapt your style a little, such as chatting to Grandma versus chatting to your friends, but that's not the same as reconstructing your personality to be liked by every room you're in.

Do you feel you change considerably depending on who you're with? Do you hold different opinions and values depending on who is standing in front of you? If so, take a moment to reflect on this now and then have a go at the exercise below.

Pop a three-minute alarm on your phone, close your eyes and breathe deeply. Use this time to reflect on the relationships you have and who you are in each. How do you differ? Which 'character' is the real you? When do you feel your truest self? When do you feel furthest away from your true self? Once the three minutes are up, shake your body out and know that if you didn't have any definitive answers then that's OK. You've made a start and we'll be helping you work further on this as we go.

Questions for self-discovery

How about I throw some questions your way, so you can begin exploring who you are?

For now, you might want to just read through these and mull them over, but it would be a great idea to get out your pen and paper at some point and take a little bit more time to answer them. (And if you'd like to dig further still then I've popped even more questions for you on my website: www.iamhollymatthews.com/findyourconfidence)

Remind yourself that these questions are intended to get you to explore who you are in *this* moment now. So this is not about who you thought you would be and certainly not about what you think everybody else needs you to be. Answer from your heart and, of course, there are no wrong answers:

- How would you describe your personality?
- What activities bring you joy (or have brought you joy in the past)?
- What places make you feel the most alive?
- What scares you?
- What are your top three strengths and weaknesses? (Don't you dare rush straight to writing out weaknesses, I see you! Name those strengths too, you beautiful human!)
- Where do you feel safest?
- What is something you would love to do in your life?
- When you feel a bit crap, what do you do to lift your mood?
- What do you need in your life (top three non-negotiables)?
- What are your top three pet peeves?
- What excites you?
- What topic would you happily protest, petition or debate with people about?
- What does success look like to you?
- What can make you go from zero to 10 quickly on the anger scale?
- What do you want more of in your life? What do you want less of?
- Who would you be if no one was watching?

I know that for some of us answering these questions will be difficult and that's fine. We may well have had a vision of who we'd have liked to be at this age and that version may not be the current reality. Take comfort from the fact that however you feel now, you've lived a full life up until this point and none of that has been wasted.

The exercise may also highlight that there is work to be done in getting to know yourself, if you find answering these questions challenging. The good news is that wherever you are right now, the fact that you're reading this book tells me that you wish to find out who you are. The more that you explore who you are, getting radically honest with yourself in the process, the more ready you will be to open your heart confidently to new experiences with other humans, which is what you deserve.

Define your ideal mate, before you start to date

As well as exploring yourself, it's also important to spend time articulating what you need and want from a romantic partner. Deciding what you want in any area of your life shows confidence and bravery. Interestingly, though, when it comes to romantic relationships, we often don't take the time to consider what kind of person we want.

Sure, if you ask somebody what their 'perfect partner' is they might give you the 'tall, dark and handsome' cliché, but many of us have never really considered the important specifics that we might need.

I also appreciate that some of you reading this will be in a relationship, but that doesn't mean that you can't start identifying the factors that are important to you. It will mean you can appreciate the things you have and it could perhaps give you some ideas for things that need to be tweaked and discussed.

Let me caveat this section by saying that society really doesn't teach us that we should think about our romantic partners in this strategic way, and women particularly have even been chastised for being 'too picky' when opening up about their wants and needs. My thoughts are this: if you don't ask for what you want then you will get whatever you are given, and this is not a life that I want for you.

I mean, imagine walking into a restaurant and not telling the waiter what it is that you want to eat. Instead of choosing based on what you like, what you had last time you visited and knowing what you *don't* like, you just accept whatever is in the kitchen. It'd never happen. So why should it be any different when it comes to relationships?

No more! From this point on, you are going to declare loudly what you want from a relationship. Here are a few tips to help get your brain working out what that is:

Let bad dates and relationships be your guide

I know this part is about deciding what you *do* want, but if you're having trouble deciphering what that is, I urge you to reflect on past experiences to help you recognise what didn't work. That way, you can then flip this round and, voilà, you will have what you do want.

Base your wants on who you are and your values

What are your most important values? Perhaps you are spiritual, ambitious or political. Maybe all three? There will be those of you for whom family is the most important value and those of you who are motivated by adventure and growth, newness and novelty. Are you an introvert or an extrovert? Are you somebody who loves the great outdoors or are you a homebody who prefers to cosy up in front of your favourite movie and snuggle on the sofa? Consider your needs in terms of connection, sexual desire, lifestyle, the type of home you would like to live in and all aspects of what a great life might look like to you. If you don't align on at least most of your values, they're probably not the person for you.

Key non-negotiables

There are always going to be certain key opinions that mean we don't get on with people. Examples of these might be around your politics, religion, whether you want children or not, money, gender roles or marriage. For me there would be certain things that I could absolutely not get past, such as anybody who was intolerant of other people particularly based on their sexuality, race or background. I couldn't be in a relationship with somebody who didn't like children or animals and I wouldn't choose to be with a partner who smoked or took drugs. These are my personal preferences and may be completely different to yours, but I'm sharing them as examples so you can see that it's safe to be specific. Knowing what your non-negotiables are can help you make very clear decisions on whether someone would fit into your life or not.

Red flags and green flags

Some of my very good friends are completely colour blind (you know who you are) and they totally ignore early signs that a potential love interest isn't going to be a great partner. A red flag is a warning that this relationship could be unhealthy, toxic or manipulative. These will be different for all of us but there are some big ones that none of us should accept, such as controlling, jealous or aggressive behaviour. Any kind of gaslighting or lying is a warning sign too, and I would consider major red flags to be if they don't have any friends outside of you, or if they don't see their child from a previous relationship. You will potentially have your own red flags that you look out for based on past negative experiences.

The flipside to this is finding green flags, which are key signs that somebody is a decent person and a potentially healthy partner. These might be that they are kind to animals, take care of their family members, are empathetic, emotionally intelligent, non-judgemental, respectful of your time or that they communicate openly.

Relationship role models

You might consider which relationships you see around you that are connected, healthy and loving. Having role models is a great idea and can help you to see another type of bond, especially if you have grown up in a home with a toxic relationship or had a past pernicious partner.

Now that we've looked at what we want, let's look at how to articulate these things in relationships or to check to see whether a person has these qualities.

Real conversation and all the communication

When you hear the word 'vulnerability', what does that bring up for you? I know that for me the idea of being vulnerable used to sound a lot like being weak. It potentially meant being walked all over or feeling exposed in some way, and I'm pretty sure that some of you reading this will relate.

I'm here to help you unpick this old idea about vulnerability though, and to support you in recognising that being vulnerable in life is the hallmark of pure confidence. If you're willing to open up about who you are and to share things that feel embarrassing or come with a fear of judgement from others, then you are strong AF.

If you currently fear vulnerability (and this might not be something that you've ever acknowledged before), it may show up for you in the form of the following:

* Never wanting to talk about anything controversial for fear of exposing yourself in some way.
* Hating the idea of dressing fancy or in anything too outlandish because you're worried that everybody would look at you and this would make you feel anxious.
* Never offering up compliments to anyone in case they rebuff you.
* Public displays of affection or declarations of love give you 'the ick'.
* Fearing standing out, making yourself known, the potential judgement and rejection if people get too close.
* Being fearful of sharing what you like because you're worried this might say something about who you are that others would judge.

These are signs that you're trying to protect your lovely heart, but by doing so you are putting up a big wall that keeps others out. If you're to have the kind of relationships you hope to have, then feeling vulnerable is something you're going to have to get used to. Love is a leap of faith and declaring that love can feel utterly terrifying.

Conversations to encourage connection

To start taking down the bricks of your walls you need to begin sharing openly and having real conversations with those whom you wish to have a relationship with. If you think back to some of the best conversations you've ever had, I bet the reason they were good was that you felt listened to, understood and both you and the other person opened up in some way.

Earlier in the chapter, we looked at understanding yourself and knowing what *you* want. You need to understand how to share this with a partner, or potential partner, and ask for your own needs to be met. In a relationship, though, you also need to know what the other person wants. The only way to do any of this is by having an honest (and sometimes uncomfortable) conversation.

If it's a brand-new relationship, then this is a fantastic opportunity to be candid and real about everybody's wants and needs, instead of creating problems later. If this is a relationship that you've been in for a while, you can still begin these conversations and revamp and refresh your connection. We aren't the same people throughout our lives and so there is always the opportunity to press pause and look at what we currently want within our relationships. Often the reason why relationships fail is because these conversations only happen when the relationship hits crisis point.

So, what kind of conversations could you be having that would support your relationship and give you the confidence to feel secure and connected? Let's take a look.

Brand-new relationships

At this stage in a relationship, it really is about having *all* the conversations there are to have. Dating is essentially an audition for both of you. You're getting to know each other and you're looking to see whether it could stand the test of time. This is hard to foresee unless you really understand the other person's background, likes, dislikes, fears and wants, so get talking! Useful topics to discuss could be*:

- **Life goals** – A chance for you to share personal goals about all aspects of your life: career, travel, education, lifestyle, hobbies, experiences and anything else that comes to mind. Perhaps you could even begin discussing joint goals.
- **Family** – This might be looking at their relationship with their own family or how they feel about family in general. If you want children and they don't then that is going to be a pretty big stopper to the relationship.
- **Non-negotiables** – The things on your own list and on your partner's list and understanding where they fit together. For example, if your partner wants to go to church every Sunday and you're an atheist, then you might be able to anticipate some future clashes.
- **Expectations** – Maybe you want to understand their expectations of you, what they constitute as cheating (which can be surprisingly nuanced for people) or their levels of jealousy. Expectations might be how they see your role in the relationship, in the home or how often they expect to be in contact with you.
- **Favourite things** – There are, of course, the obvious fun questions around their favourite things to do, watch, listen to and enjoy.

---

* A quick disclaimer: these deep conversations are probably not first-date material, although I'll leave you to use your own judgement about when it feels appropriate to have them.

- **Deeper questions** – Don't be scared to ask more difficult questions though, such as if they feel comfortable saying sorry when they are wrong, how they respond when they are angry, sad or frustrated, and how they might like to be supported if and when they feel like this.

Long-term established relationships

Just because you've been in a relationship for a while doesn't mean that you can't introduce new conversations. These might look like some of the topics below:

- **How you share and receive love** – Talking about ways that you share and receive love is a brave conversation and can really help us to make our partner feel special and connected. I often joke that if I share song lyrics, memes or funny videos with you, I most definitely love you. I also understand that I'm a very explicit person who needs to hear words, rather than just receiving the actions (this may be to do with my neurodivergence). There will be other people who don't need to hear the words 'I love you' but need to *feel* that love in the form of touch, being taken care of or even through food. There should be no judgement in how we do this, just an understanding of our preferred way of communicating.
- **How you deal with difficulty or conflict** – It's also useful to understand how somebody copes in times of conflict. For instance, I know that in an argument I have the tendency to keep going until I find a resolution. If the other person needs time to process what has been said, then my way of communicating is likely to be unhelpful. Equally, if I don't know that the other person needs time to process, I may misunderstand their stepping-back as a rejection. If we understand what we both need ahead of time, then that pre-established rule can help us both feel confident and secure in getting a positive outcome.
- **Check-ins** – It's important to regularly check in with what everybody needs in their lives and within the relationship

itself. This might even be something that you create as a weekly, daily or monthly conversation. It's much better to have those conversations as you go than to get a shock at the end of the year when somebody unexpectedly announces something radical.

- **The past** – It's healthy to share old stories, what makes you who you are and any triggers that you're aware of that may show up (or perhaps already have) within the relationship. These may include experiences such as divorce, bereavement, illness and traumatic relationships or events, all of which shape the person who is in the relationship today. If your partner isn't aware of this stuff, they may unintentionally stand on an emotional landmine that they had zero understanding was ever there.

Some general sentence templates like the ones below may also give you some ideas:

- When you do ... it makes me feel like...
- When I do ... I would like it if you...
- When I am anxious ... I would like it if you...
- When I am angry ... it would help me if you would...
- When you don't ... I feel...
- I love it when you...
- Show me love by...

A word of warning: when you start doing this work on your confidence and having these conversations, it is very likely that the other person in the relationship will have questions and potentially find this challenging. If you have accepted certain behaviours up until this point, and you have had fewer boundaries or open conversations, your partner may need time to adjust. Don't take this as an indication that you should stop working on your confidence and your assertiveness within a relationship, just notice (with compassion) that your person will need time to find their new normal.

The confidence to disagree, say no, get hurt and let go

Imagine that your partner has a bow and arrow, and they're practising archery. You are holding the target and running around the field trying to catch that arrow for them (because they aren't very good at archery). You're out of breath, you're running from one place to another, but you're so worried that they might feel bad about their lack of skill and you so desperately want them to love you, that you're nearly breaking your neck to accommodate them. Obviously, this analogy is far-fetched but there are some of you in relationships who are metaphorically doing exactly this: papering over cracks, running around all over the place and putting yourself at the bottom of the list of priorities. So why do we do this?

American psychiatrist Aaron Beck shared that we do this because we often have overly rigid and unrealistic expectations for our social interactions and we're overly invested in acceptance from other people. Beck created a scale that people can use to indicate where they sit on the spectrum, from sociotropy (an excessive investment in your interpersonal relationships, e.g. people pleasing) to autonomy (the ability to make an informed, uncoerced decision about your life). Individuals who appear closer to sociotropy have much higher levels of anxiety and lower self-esteem than their counterparts who are closer to autonomy. This is another reminder of what happens when we give away our power.

The problem with people pleasing

When I work with clients, I'll often get kickback when I discuss people-pleasing tendencies, as they'll tell me that their behaviour is just 'being kind'. They defend their actions as that of a loving partner, and although they admit to being burnt-out, it's OK because they love that person and it's 'nice to be nice'.

Erm, let's unpack that for a moment. There is a huge difference between being altruistic and people pleasing. People pleasing comes with a side order of anxiety, a fear of saying no, worry about getting hurt, fear of being rejected and a fear of conflict. There is also the potential feeling of loneliness, because while we are moulding ourselves to fit everybody else's needs, we are essentially creating a character and that character feels disconnected from our real essence. Going back to the archery analogy, you are essentially a moving target that your partner can't get to know.

If our behaviour is altruism and coming from a place of being genuinely nice, that would only come from us when we're feeling energised. We act altruistically when our cup is so full that we can dish out love and time, giving it away like candy. There is no anxiety and there is no fear driving this behaviour; it's just a lovely gesture and act of giving.

As I've said many times in this chapter, a good relationship is about both people getting their needs met, and you are also 'people'. If you want to get your needs met, then this means putting boundaries in place and articulating your needs. Let's look at this now.

Setting healthy boundaries

The antidote to people pleasing is as follows: assertiveness, having autonomy over your life and setting boundaries. Rather than bellowing at yourself to 'stop people pleasing!' let's start celebrating when we're assertive and setting healthy boundaries. By praising ourselves for the win (being assertive) rather than chastising the old behaviour (people pleasing), we are far more likely to see a change.

Nathaniel Brandon is a leading voice in the world of self-esteem and he wrote a powerful book called *The Six Pillars of Self-esteem* (1995). Self-responsibility and self-assertiveness are two of these key pillars. If we consider these in the realm of our relationships, then self-responsibility is about understanding what we want and knowing that it is our personal responsibility to create the foundation to have this. Self-assertiveness is our ability to articulate to other people what we want and create strong boundaries to support this.

Setting a boundary and saying no, for some of us, is going to feel like an alien concept, and that's OK, that's why we're here. Boundary setting and self-esteem are happy bedfellows and people with high self-esteem most definitely feel comfortable setting boundaries.

Here is a three-step guide to setting boundaries that will help you get clear and take action (and if you'd like more then revisit the section on boundaries on p. 96):

Step 1: Wake up – Grab a pen and paper and take some notes. Articulate your boundaries to yourself, know your limits and your 'hard nos' and spend some time understanding what you need. Consider boundaries in terms of physical, emotional, time, material, sexual and financial needs. Respect yourself enough to understand that you are allowed to say no, you are allowed to have an opinion and, even if you love somebody, you are allowed to disagree with them. Write your boundaries down so you're clear on them before taking the next step.

Step 2: Speak up – Clearly and firmly communicate what your boundary is to your partner, and the consequences of a breach. For example, 'I feel respected when you arrive on time for dinner, and I would like it if you would say when you are running behind. If you are late without letting me know, I will eat dinner without you.' Using 'I statements' is a great tool to make sure the other person doesn't feel under attack because you're making it clear that this is about you and your feelings. It might help to practise what you're going to say beforehand so you feel confident in your wording.

Step 3: Stand up – If you're in a relationship with somebody who continuously ignores your boundaries then there may come a time when you walk away. This is never an easy decision but if you have explored all other avenues of communication, this may be the only option left. The most confident version of you will walk away from relationships where there is no respect left. On my website (www.iamhollymatthews.com/findyourconfidence), I have given you a list of examples of things you can say to the people in your life who consistently break your boundaries.

As with all conversations, it is important to choose the right moment to have them. Screaming your demands over dinner with the family is not likely to get the outcome that you want. Request, don't complain, listen to the other person and don't be afraid to apologise when you get things wrong. The confidence to have such big conversations and set strong boundaries will at times feel exhausting. Make sure that you're taking care of yourself and seeking support when needed.

The importance of friends

A slightly depressing fact I heard recently (based on research done by Professor Robin Dunbar, an evolutionary psychologist at the University of Oxford) was that when we get into a relationship, we lose on average two close friends. The research showed that our romantic relationship will take the place of the close bonds we had prior to its existence. If I look to my own friendship circle, this sadly has often rung true.

So what's the problem with losing some friendships for the sake of romantic love? Well, when we eradicate relationships that we had prior to our romantic ones, this can often manifest itself in us then expecting more of our partners. We might find that we begin putting undue expectations on them, expecting them to fill the void we've created by having less of a life outside of this companionship.

Do you fall into this pattern? If you notice that you tend to go 'all in' on a romantic relationship (at the expense of other relationships), then start exploring what you can do to support some change. This might mean that you begin rekindling old friendships or perhaps it's just something to be mindful of when you do enter a romantic relationship again. There's no expiration date on reaching out to an old friend. Just start right now... I dare you to text that old mate!

Also, it's worth knowing that having friendships and interests outside of your relationship can actually allow the relationship to thrive. Research conducted by Dr Terri Orbuch, a psychologist and author of *Finding Love Again: 6 Simple Steps to a New and Happy Relationship* (2012) tells us that space and privacy are more important to us in a long-term relationship than a good sex life. Orbuch began her study into marriage and divorce in 1990 and it now has long-term research from over 740 individuals across different racial backgrounds.

So, why do we need space from our romantic partners? Well, Orbuch's study revealed that when partners have their own set of interests, hobbies and friends it stops them from being bored in their relationships. It allows the couple space to process their thoughts, helps them keep their sense of 'I' and promotes strength, independence and a freshness within that relationship. Confidence and self-esteem in a relationship means knowing that even though you want that person in your life, you would be OK if they weren't there too. So there you have it: keeping your mates close is actually good for your romantic relationships – what a bonus! Let's finish, as always, with some action points to build on what we've discussed.

Create a confident vibe and watch love thrive

To help you put into practice the techniques we've discussed in this chapter, here are some action points to get you started.

Inside:

1 **Know what you'd like, so love can strike.** This is the time to grab your pen and paper and write out your 'love list' of ingredients that you need in a romantic partner. If you're single, this list is a way to get clear and focused on exactly what you want and if you are already in a relationship it can help you appreciate your partner's good qualities or else realise when a relationship may no longer be serving you. Don't censor this list; it's just for you and you deserve a great list.

2 **Ditch trying to get hitched.** Before a date, set an intention for yourself. This doesn't have to be a heavy intention such as 'find the partner of my dreams and get married next month', as this will likely make you nervous and the situation feel more intense. Instead, try something like 'I would like to enjoy my evening and have a great conversation.' Releasing the expectations of 'perfect' will lessen your nerves and allow you space to get to know your companion without any pressure.

3 **Believe what you can't yet see.** Relationships are about trust and although it's important for us to take action towards the things we want, we have to be mindful of letting go of past negative experiences to give ourselves permission to believe in better. Listen to the language that you use around relationships and see where you can change your internal dialogue to feel more positive. 'I attract losers into my life' could be shifted to 'I *used to* attract losers into my life but that's an old story.' The phrase 'I'll never find love' could be changed to 'Now that I know myself, love and connection come easily.'

Outside:

1 **Practise asking questions and listening.** With your 'love list' to hand and your detective hat firmly on, play around with speaking the questions you'd like to ask out loud. Remember that this isn't a job interview, and you certainly don't want to fire questions at them at machine-gun speed, but know that you'll feel more confident if this is not the first time you've said the words. You can also practise difficult conversations you may want to have about boundary setting within your relationship. Practise pausing and giving space – knowing that this is not a monologue and that the other person will also have their own questions.

2 **Fancy attire, inner fire!** What we wear inevitably impacts how we feel and helps us cement our identity at that time. On a date, I encourage you to wear something that you feel great in. That doesn't mean wearing something that you think you *should* wear but something you *want* to wear. If we choose from a place of 'should', then we're simply playing a character and going against the things that we've learned in this chapter. For those in a relationship, wearing something different and freshening up your style can help to build your self-esteem and switch how your partner sees you.

3 **Your body talks.** Try to avoid defensive body language such as folded arms, clenched fists, a rigid posture or facing your body away from your date or partner. Be mindful, both when in a relationship (and discussing the relationship or setting boundaries) and while on a date, of submissive body language, such as hiding your hands (by sitting on them or holding them behind your back) or looking down and avoiding eye contact. Watch out for becoming a 'bobble head' and nodding continuously as they speak, talking very quietly or rolling your shoulders forward. These are all key indicators that you feel unconfident.

Positive and confident body language to support you looks like:

- sitting or standing up straight;
- shoulders back;
- genuinely smiling and looking the other person in the eye;

- open gestures when talking, and leaning in towards your date or partner as this can demonstrate that you are interested in what they have to say;
- subtly mirroring body language, which can help you to build some rapport (see more on mirroring on p. 68);
- nodding three times as they speak as a way of showing your engagement and agreement.

Remember, while positive body language can be practised and learned, don't become so rigid in what you're doing that you feel inauthentic in your interactions. Make sure you're focused on your date or partner and be responsive to their cues. For more resources on body language, head to www.iamhollymatthews.com/findyourconfidence.

Guest advice

Persia Lawson
Dating and relationship coach
@persialawson

"The key to true confidence in dating and relationships is to stop looking outside of yourself for the partner you want to GET, and start looking inside of yourself for the partner you want to BE."

#7

Parenting

My head pounded and my cheeks flushed. I was propped up by pillows on a hospital bed and could hear the clattering of the ward echoing around me.

I was 34 and a half weeks pregnant and had woken up that morning with a painful headache that I just couldn't shift. I had nonchalantly called my midwife and now found myself waiting in hospital for a doctor to prescribe (what I assumed) would be 'home and rest', ready for my next check-up in a week's time. A doctor had been in my room a few moments earlier but then alarms went off in another patient's room and he was whisked out before he could explain anything to me.

A nurse casually strolled into my room and said, 'So it looks like we will be having this baby in the next few days. I'll get you moved on to the ward in the next half an hour and it's probably best your husband goes and gets your bag.'

What?! I had at least six weeks left, didn't I?

My husband Ross and I glanced at each other with a mixture of fear, excitement and confusion. I now knew I was about to become a parent a lot sooner than I had imagined, and I should probably start reading some of those books on 'how to be a parent' that people had gifted me.

My stumble into parenthood came with the same calamity of events that many parents experience when their baby is finally ready to arrive (no birth story is ever the same and they nearly all have a twist or two in the tale). On 15 March 2011, my tiny baby girl, Brooke Blair, arrived in this world and changed my life forever. Just a few short years later, and with her own chaotic arrival, I was incredibly lucky to have my second daughter, Texas Blair, who completed my sassy duo.

At the age of 29, I had two tiny humans who were relying on me to guide them in this world. For every new parent, this is an exciting new adventure (and one hell of a lot of pressure!).

It's OK if we don't know what we are doing

When we are young and we see adults with children, we assume that those adults feel self-assured and in control. We look at them safe in the knowledge that they know what they're doing, and that if we were to find ourselves becoming parents in the future, then we too would know what to do. We would ease into this blissful state of parental 'knowing', just as they had.

Now here's the secret that I'd like to gift to any future parents (or to anyone who spends time around other parents): this state of 'knowing' never comes. Nobody who is or has been a parent really has a clue what they're doing. Yes, this includes that mum on the PTA who organises the fete and made goodie bags for all the kids at the end of term. It includes your parents, your neighbours, your doctor and that couple who you went to school with who post gorgeous aspirational pictures of their seemingly neat and tidy family as they travel the globe.

This might scare you or it might make you feel seen, depending on your personal circumstances. But either way, humans have been navigating this truth way longer than our lifetimes, and they will continue to do so for many moons after.

Parenting is different every single day and I don't think I really recognised, before becoming a parent, the way that this would challenge me or how completely ill-equipped it would make me feel at times. Every year, every milestone and each child are different, and the lessons I have to learn seem to never stop.

Now let me make this very clear from the start that this is *not* a parenting advice chapter. Based on mine and the majority of my clients' experience, I will focus on motherhood, but this advice includes all genders of parents and will hopefully be helpful for non-parents and 'cool aunties' too. I am not going to tell you how to best parent or start pontificating about the new in-vogue style of 'rearing your young'. What we will talk about, though, is the rarely discussed 'symptom' of becoming a parent, the one many of us have to 'treat' throughout our lives: a lack of confidence.

I went into being a parent with the cocksure swagger of youth and ignorance. I hadn't been around young children much and was never the one who cooed over babies. I also happened to be the first out of my friendship group to become a parent (which I think was a shock to most people), meaning I had zero understanding of what parenthood would entail.

My ignorance when it came to parenting included me not knowing the 'secret' that no parent ever feels completely in control. So, I didn't see my own confidence dip coming. And then WHAM, my cavalier and cocksure demeanour disappeared and I was catapulted into a constant state of dread. I began to worry I simply wasn't good enough to parent. I feared I would damage my children forever if I dared to stick them in front of *Peppa Pig* while I made a cuppa or didn't sterilise their bottles correctly.

Why did I feel like this? I was a confident woman in many situations. I could happily stand in front of an audience without a blink or stride into a new class without breaking a sweat, and yet here I was, terrified of looking after these miniature people.

For many of us who have experienced this lack of confidence in parenting, you may find that it sneaks up on you. It might even build in momentum for a time (until you begin to acknowledge it). If this is you now, then this is your gentle nudge to begin to address it and gift yourself the tools you need. You deserve this.

I first want us to recognise that feeling unconfident in parenting is totally normal. In fact, not only is it normal, but if you *weren't* concerned at all, then *this* would concern me. Being concerned means that you care. It means that you take your responsibility as a parent seriously, so you should be proud of yourself for this.

> **'Being concerned means that you care.** It means that you take your **responsibility as a parent seriously**, so you should **be proud of yourself** for this.'

Reframe the guilt and fear with the recognition that these feelings mean you continue to work on being the best parent you can be, every day, and that's awesome. *You* are awesome. Plus, you don't need to worry because throughout this chapter I'm going to give you lots of support to help you build that confidence and self-esteem right back up.

Off-the-cuff and good enough

I open a bag that is stuffed to the brim and peel something out. If you squint, this 'something' can be recognised as my daughter's PE kit. It's 8 a.m. and she leaves the house in 10 minutes' time. She has PE today and this crumpled tracksuit has mud from last week's rugby lesson sprayed across it.

Yes, she should have put it in the washing basket. Yes, it's her responsibility. BUT it's also my job as a parent to keep an eye on that, so as I stand in my kitchen hovering between rage and guilt, I get to work.

A bodge job of washing-up liquid, a scour and a whole lot of elbow grease later, and the mud is off and my daughter is at school. This is one incident in a whole long line of moments when I have had to go for 'good enough', and I'm going to share why I believe these moments can be pivotal in whether our confidence is lowered or strengthened.

If we look at this moment as an example, I could lower my confidence by berating myself in my head: 'Why didn't I remember to check her PE bag?' and 'Why do I always forget things?' and 'I bet the other parents at the school have their child's PE kit all neatly ironed in their drawers.' (Caveat: most probably don't.)

Or I could choose to see what happened as a positive. Sure, I forgot to wash the PE kit, but I worked off-the-cuff in the moment. I problem-solved and I got stuff done. I can now view myself as a parent who can fix, sort and be relied upon to never let you down (even when I kind of have let you down initially!).

You see being 'good enough' when it comes to most areas of our parenting leaves us with space to be *incredible* in other areas of our parenting.

Circle of Security International is a parenting organisation that definitely supports the idea of 'good enough'. The company runs parenting programmes internationally to support parents in understanding their child's needs, and in becoming confident parents. They recognise that the core principles of being a great parent include being there to support your child going out in the world (cheering them on, delighting in their achievements and joy) and being there when your child is coming in, back to the domestic setting (supporting them emotionally and helping them to navigate their emotions).

I like Circle of Security's way of breaking down parenting as I feel it simplifies the job in a way that makes it feel less overwhelming. Ultimately, it's about being 'with your child' in it all, without pouring judgement on yourself, giving yourself the freedom to do things your own way and simply aiming for good enough.

So, what does good enough actually look like on a daily basis?

- Good enough means dropping the ball sometimes.
- Good enough means getting it wrong sometimes.
- Good enough means forgetting its non-uniform day, running your children back to the car, where your good-enough effort at emptying the car last week means there's non-uniform clothes left in the boot, so you can quickly change your kids before ushering them back into school like you forgot nothing.
- Good enough means a messy house.
- Good enough means forgetting to arrange a grocery delivery (it's beans on toast tonight again, girls!).
- Good enough means running into your child's school assembly 10 minutes late with dripping wet hair because you were in the shower when you remembered you were supposed to be there. Still getting there … just drenched and late (and yes, this is a personal story).
- Good enough is whatever works for you and your family to allow you permission to let some things go. (And I would love to hear your good-enough moments as I bet some are hilarious. Do send them over on Instagram @iamhollymatthews if you want to share!)

Ultimately, 'good enough' is a much more realistic goal than 'perfect' and research even shows that going for good enough can make us happier. Let's take a look.

The research

In the 1950s, American psychologist Herbert Simon coined the names 'satisficers' and 'maximisers' as a way of determining how people respond to 'choice'. If you are a 'maximiser' then you are more likely to spend time deliberating and trying to perfect your choices. 'Satisficers' on the other hand are more likely to go for the good-enough option. There have been many studies to show that where we sit between the two impacts our mental health.

Barry Schwartz, a psychology professor and author of *The Paradox of Choice* (2005), is a big fan of being a 'satisficer'. He believes that the single most important thing parents can do is to teach their kids that 'good enough' is almost always 'good enough', and that if we always model 'only the best will do' then we teach our kids the same lesson. He concludes from his own studies that satisficers are simply happier. Why is this?

There are pros and cons to both, of course (and more details of these different studies can be found on my website), but those who lean towards life as a 'maximiser' are more likely to be categorised as a 'perfectionist'. People with perfectionist tendencies can have higher levels of regret, dissatisfaction, depression and rumination.

Maximisers can also often find themselves comparing and contrasting options at an exhausting rate and, because being a parent comes with thousands of tiny decisions to be made on a daily basis, this can be a challenge. How we choose to respond to the choices laid out in front of us will ultimately shift our mood and levels of self-esteem. Approaching the daily parenting choices with a maximiser approach of 'I have to make the perfect choice or I've failed' will most likely lead to a long-term lowering of your self-esteem versus the satisficer approach of 'I'll do my best and that's OK.'

What do I mean by this? Well, if I look at the parenting choices I have had to make just this week, for example, they include: my children's bedtimes; what they eat every day; how many snacks are too many; how much screen time is too much; whether I should allow my daughter to stay at her friend's house; and whether I need to implement a chore chart to get my youngest to *finally* start bringing her dirty dishes downstairs. This is on top of the constant micro 'should I say this' or 'should I do that' that is part of daily life.

Being a parent comes with so many choices that if we were to 'maximise' every decision then we would quickly burn out. In addition, our feelings around not being able to do everything at 'maximiser' standard would likely dent our fragile confidence.

A case study on expectations

During lockdown life back in 2020, many of us got hooked on the same things. There was *Tiger King*, TikTok dances and banana bread galore, and one of these lockdown-life boredom-killers was Marie Kondo.

Marie Kondo (for those who managed to not succumb to folding clothes in that very special Marie Kondo way) is a Japanese organising consultant, TV presenter and author who has sold millions of copies of her books worldwide. In her Netflix series *Tidying Up with Marie Kondo* she goes into people's homes and helps them get organised. One of her tactics for helping people with their mounds of stuff was to take each item and get the person to ask themselves honestly if the item 'sparked joy' in their life. The person would then hold that item, notice if joy was sparked and, if not, they would thank that item for being part of their life and it would be sent to the charity shop or recycling bin.

As with most things in my life, I spent a whole day going far too deep into trying out this new fad. This involved decluttering my home, asking my orange sequinned boob tube if it sparked joy for me, and then recognising that it had never been worn, so holding it close, thanking it and throwing it in a pile on the floor with gusto.

My drawers were organised, bags for charity were at the door and as the sun set, I began to come out of my Marie Kondo haze. It was then that I realised the house was still a mess. I'd not eaten, done any work or drunk any water, was late making dinner, and I knew, in my heart, that my drawers would be crammed with joyless clothes again soon.

Now I am not discounting the good in the 'Konmarie' method and I know she has helped many millions of people across the globe. However, as a parent, decluttering in this way just seems like an impossible extra task to take on (I mean, let's be real here, you might be pushing your luck if you try to get your moody teenager to play by the 'sparking joy' rules).

Therefore, I'm fairly confident in guessing that there were a few of you (like me) who found Marie Kondo's teachings rather unrealistic, and some who maybe even felt a little judged by the approach. Well, hold the phone! The messy-homed parents among us have been vindicated recently as the Queen of Tidy herself came out and admitted that after having had three children she has 'kind of given up' on having a tidy home. Hallelujah! Yes! We knew it!

Now my point in sharing this here is not to feel smug about Marie Kondo's admission – I promise! Instead, it's to make the point that our expectations of ourselves have a huge part to play in how we feel internally. If we have such high standards that we try to perfect *every* area of our life, we then run the risk of lowering our self-esteem when we fall short of these impossibly high expectations.

This doesn't mean having no standards or not going for gold in some areas, but parents have so much to do that we have to let ourselves drop the ball on occasion, without judging ourselves for it.

Moment to pause
Let's all take a nice breath in and a delicious sigh out (I love a big sigh!). Consider whether your expectations of yourself might be on the fantasy standards end of the scale. If that's the case, then have a think about whether there might be some areas of your life where you can turn down the pressure and let go of the burden to be perfect.

How to deal with the opinions of others

One reason we often have such high standards for ourselves is fear of judgement if we happen to have a parenting 'fail' or fall short in any way. Therefore, tackling how to cope with the opinions of others in a parenting context is what we'll look at next.

In the feral wasteland of social media, we have been conditioned to expect the opinions of other people and to also give our own. Every second of the day, there is a keyboard warrior telling someone else why the way they are living their life isn't correct and giving them advice or instructions on how they should change.

On becoming a parent, you step aggressively into this quagmire of opinions and advice. This advice is very often as unsolicited as it comes. You will have strangers in the street chastising you for your child being barefoot in their pushchair (even though you've put their damn socks back on every few metres for the past hour and only just decided to give up).

You'll have Great-aunt Margaret telling you that 'allowing' your young boy to play with dolls is going to impact his sexuality (a note here: Great-aunt Margaret is talking nonsense, let your boys play!). It's whether to breastfeed or not to breastfeed; to co-sleep or put them in their own room. Do you batch-cook nutritious food from the veg you grew in your allotment or grab a pre-made jar of pesto from the supermarket and throw it on some pasta for the third night in a row? There are so many thoughts and opinions on parenting that it will make your head spin.

When there is so much 'advice' on offer it's easy to see how, as a parent, you might get lost and begin to distrust your own opinion.

Well, let me offer this as my own take on it: *you* know *your* child better than anyone else. You likely spend the most time with them and they don't know anything other than how you do things. There is always going to be more than one way to bring up a child and that doesn't mean right or wrong, just different. If that is the case, then we can conclude that *your* way of doing things will be just as great as the next person's, and we will all do good and bad things throughout this journey.

At this point I think it's important for us to look at why we decide to make the choices that we do as parents. What is the driving force behind our decision making?

What your parents did

Well, first, let's think of our own experience of having been parented. Either we think our parents or caregivers did a fabulous job and we wish to emulate this; we think they failed miserably and we dragged ourselves up (in which case you're probably actively trying to do the exact opposite to what you experienced); or you sit somewhere in the middle, recognising it was a little of both. Whichever is true, your own early life is shaping your current parenting style, whether you wish to confront this or not.

When you were born

Our decisions will be based on the era in which we grew up. Parenting advice has changed dramatically over the years (and no doubt will continue to do so). Looking back with fresh eyes it can be horrifying to see some of the advice that was given in the past. Let's have some fun and look at some examples of this together now.

In the early 20th century, the tome *A Handbook of Obstetric Nursing* (1902) gave the advice that women should not snuggle or kiss their babies as it would 'foolishly spoil them' and mean they would bring up 'little tyrants'.

In 1928, the child behaviourist John Watson took this a step further in his manual *Psychological Care of the Infant and Child* (1928) by suggesting women must be 'sensible' with how much they interact with their children, if at all. He offered up the guidance that women mustn't hug or kiss their infants, nor let them sit on their laps. They could shake their hands or pat them on the heads in the morning and, at a push, kiss them on their foreheads before they went to sleep.

A few decades later, Walter Sacket wrote in his parenting manual *Bringing up Babies* (1962) that we should be weaning babies on to solid foods at two days old. By three months of age, the baby would be eating bacon and eggs and by six months old, chugging down a coffee (I assume by the time they hit one they're smoking a pipe and off to work?).

I'm sure that you are as appalled as I am at reading some of this outdated advice, but I'm afraid to say that there will be things we are doing right now that will scandalise future generations, too. So, when someone of a different generation offers their wisdom, it's not to say they're always wrong, but it's to remind ourselves that their understanding is likely based on what they did 'in their day'.

Your values

You will also base the way in which you parent on what your values are, and that makes how you parent incredibly unique (and so it should be).

Your values are the 'ingredients' that matter to you in creating a life that feels good. You will have certain values that you attribute specifically to parenting, and others that you hold dear overall. In terms of parenting, you might really value freedom for your children and feel that this trumps rules and rigidity, for example. Or perhaps you feel that honesty is an integral part of your parenting journey or instilling good manners into your child. The larger values, for some, may be based on a particular religion, culture or perhaps even a political ideology. These act as a kind of compass and help to guide us through our lives. Even now as I list a few examples here, it is easy to see how this can bring about conflict with others as our values collide.

I have always felt it is important that my children get choice in what they wear. If I look back on my own childhood, there were times when there was a level of strictness over my clothing (although this waned as I got older). So my 'loosey goosey' attitude to my children's dress sense is perhaps based on this. I also believe that what we wear reflects who we wish to be, and choosing clothing is a fun and creative experience that helps us understand ourselves.

If you were to speak to my sister, however, she would likely regale you with 'horror' stories of what my children have turned up wearing to her house, as her parenting style regarding clothing is very different – she's far more traditional in this sense. There's no judgement on this, and in this example it's highly unlikely either of our approaches is going to dramatically impact our children. However, it's easy to see how even among siblings the difference *could* create drama.

The great thing about knowing what your values are, though, is that when people offer advice or opinions you can check in with your list of 'What values are important to me as a parent?' If the advice doesn't sit within your framework, then you can discard it and move on (without worrying that this difference in opinion means you are in the wrong).

This doesn't, of course, mean that you never listen to anyone else, and there will be lessons learned along the way that can change our values over time. The things I thought I might do as a parent, for example, have turned out to be rather different than I expected (based on what has happened in my life to date) and that's OK. Listen to advice in the right places but always check in with your own values and moral compass as you grow and change.

It's also a rather pointless exercise to get offended every time someone imparts their wisdom, because for the most part, people are doing so for the right reasons (even if they're wrong or not in keeping with how you wish to parent).

Since my husband Ross died, I have had lots of advice about how my children need a man around for discipline. The 'offerors' have pontificated that any time my children's behaviour hasn't been its best, it is down to this factor. I have at times had to grit my teeth, know what I was experiencing and trust myself, which – as is the case for any of us – can be hard when the stakes feel so high. It turns out that one of my daughters is autistic and some of the things that were being put down to needing a 'firm hand' and 'a dominant male voice' were in fact traits of her autism and being dysregulated.

> "Listen to advice in the right places but **always check in with your own values** and moral compass as you grow and change."

Now those who offered up this kind of advice to me weren't doing so from a place of judgement or dislike for me, they were doing so based on their knowledge of the world and what had probably worked for them. They were trying to help me find solutions and their intentions were good, so if I had been reactionary in the face of this, it would have been unhelpful.

At the end of this chapter, I am going to share with you some questions to help you work out what your personal parenting values might be. Knowing these is going to help you trust the decisions you make about the choices that will fall into your lap as a parent. You will then be confident when deciding 'Does this make sense for what I hope for my child?' and 'Does this seem like a good choice based on my model of the world and the values I hold dear?' Having your values in mind can help you feel confident stepping forward into being the best parent you can.

How to deal with parenting guilt

I finally manage to slump myself down on to my sofa with a cup of tea in hand, another long day of parenting under my belt. I pick up my phone and go in for my usual Russian roulette of nightly scrolling. I see pictures of other mums and their children, I see the successes of other business owners, perhaps I catch something funny that I share with my sister on WhatsApp. My mind buzzes with the information I'm being fed.

Along the way, I shall likely make assumptions about other people's posts, perhaps deciding what I like and don't like about what they're sharing. If I'm not careful, I shall begin comparing myself to some of these posts and perhaps wondering what I should be doing differently. On occasion, I have found myself following 'parenting experts' and thus, in my exhausted nightly scroll, have begun listening to their advice and feeling (for want of a better description) pretty crap about myself.

Why?

GUILT.

I feel guilt because of all the expectation and advice I am now privy to. Guilt because 'maybe they're doing it better' (they look like they are!). Guilt for working when the kids want my attention, guilt for giving them my time when I 'should' be working. Guilt for the dinner I made that possibly wasn't my best work, guilt for being a shouty mum today, and guilt for the list of many, many other reasons I know we've all likely felt as parents.

I don't know a parent out there who hasn't succumbed, at some point, to this quilt of guilt, and it can feel heavy. The stories we concoct in our minds as a result of this guilt can be another dangerous destroyer of our confidence. Let's explore this further.

Firstly, if we haven't done anything wrong, we most definitely should not feel 'guilty'. But the guilt we often do feel is essentially the consequence of all the 'shoulds' we tell ourselves are essential. You tell yourself you 'should' be enjoying the teddy bears' picnic in your kitchen (even though it's running into its third hour and your coffee has worn off); you 'should' have a tidy house (even though your three-year-old had a playdate that afternoon and you'll be picking raisins out of your shaggy rug for the rest of your life); you 'should' be able to focus on work when the kids go to bed (even though you're emotionally depleted and physically exhausted). Then there are the contradictory messages: you 'should' go back to work *and* stay at home; go to the gym but focus on your child; look incredible while also being an engaged parent or caregiver. 'Should, should, should-y should, should', all day long, and the impact is horrific guilt.

Once the guilt is there, our inner critic is sure to show up with her cruel tirade of reasons why we aren't good enough and never will be. Perhaps shame takes a seat at the table too, and soon we find ourselves stuck in a place where our self-esteem as parents is under the table on the floor. What a fun cycle of events!

Let's make guilt out of fashion with a heap of self-compassion

Let me tell you that parenting has enough stuff going on already without us adding to that pressure ourselves. I want you to step into the role of 'parenting powerhouse' with confidence, and I promise to be there to hold your hand while you do. You're not alone and I won't make it an overwhelming process.

So, start with identifying your focus. What are you consistently telling yourself about your parenting? What do you pay most attention to when it comes to parenting? What area of being a parent have you zoomed right in on and created a whole BS story around? Is it that you are worried about not having the money to do some of the things you see some parents do and you've created a story of guilt around this? Have you found yourself obsessing over food and worrying that you can't get your four-year-old to eat enough greens? Or is it just a big, fat 'I'm not good enough!' that keeps you up at night?

I want you to listen to the noise over the next few days and notice where your attention is pulled towards. Make a list of the worry thoughts that get conjured up by the things you focus on and any guilt that is attached.

For example, this week I shouted at my daughter. She burst into my bedroom at 11.30 p.m., turned my light on and jumped on my bed (as I was quite peacefully watching TV). On the one hand, me shouting is the consequence of her 'guerrilla attack' as I wound down for the day, but on the other hand, my daughter was anxious and completely emotionally dysregulated and that was her way of expressing this to me (so me being patient was needed).

In an instance like this I feel horribly guilty. The thoughts cascade from my mind about how I've ruined her life, I'm the worst parent in the world and I should be put in the stocks and have rotten fruit thrown at me. The guilt is horrific. I have, however, learned an antidote to this feeling, and I don't gatekeep what I find, so I shall share this method with you:

The antidote to guilt is self-compassion.

Recognising that you and I are human, that sometimes we respond from a place of fear, anxiety and our past experiences being triggered. That sometimes even with the best intentions in the world, we make mistakes, drop the ball and completely eff it up on occasion. And that's OK.

Being gentle with yourself doesn't mean not learning, changing and tweaking and it most definitely does not exempt you from apologising and admitting any *real* wrongdoings. Being gentle allows our moments of humanness to not chip away at our self-esteem and stops us from creating beliefs within us of not being enough.

So, what practical things can we do to practise this self-compassion? Well, I'm about the day-to-day, the tiny moments where we don't push ourselves as parents down the list of priorities. Let's look for ways in your day when you can give yourself a metaphorical (or actual) hug. It's important. This might look like:

- **Being aware of our negative self-talk** and practising 'release yourself' statements. Throughout the day you might find yourself being critical of something you've done. Let's say you're me and you snapped at your child for tearing into your room like a tornado. As guilt threatens to take you down, I want you to try a 'release yourself' statement. These could include: 'It's OK that you feel frustrated'; 'You are human, and your reaction was that of a human'; or 'You made a mistake, apologised, explained, now go back to patience and remind yourself that 90 per cent of the time she sees your love.' These statements are a beautiful, tender way of coaching yourself throughout your day and helping you to move forward.
- **Preparing your food as you might for a very prestigious guest.** That means not eating the kids' leftovers or missing meals altogether. Every time we haphazardly chuck food on a plate and maybe even eat it standing up (I see you!) we send the brain signals that this is all we deserve.

- **Giving yourself permission to stop and take a break.** I know I'm not alone in finding this a challenge, but I also know that without breaks our bodies will bring us down anyway in the form of burn-out, exhaustion and stress. So how about implementing moments to pause throughout your day, just as we're doing in this book. A moment to take time for yourself and have a cup of tea. I'm not saying it must be hours and I know you have actual, tangible stuff you need to do, but not allowing yourself a break at all will eventually slow you down for longer, so take it seriously.

- **Getting the health checks you need.** Sadly, too many parents put off health checks, doctors' appointments and even picking up prescriptions because they feel too busy and give everyone else their attention. Esther Hodges, a mum from Barnet in London, shared her tragic story in the UK press recently about how she put off a cervical screening for 13 years because she was 'too busy'. Sadly, when she finally did go, she was diagnosed with incurable cancer. This is an utter tragedy, but if we aren't careful, it could be any one of us. Book that appointment and get things checked.

- **Taking care to dress in a way that makes you feel good.** Do your hair and your make-up (if that's your thing) and get dressed in clothes that make you feel like 'you'. You'll be amazed at the difference this can make to your self-esteem. You're still a person in your own right too, alongside being a parent, and you deserve to show up in the world as yourself.

- **Saying no to things that don't support your values or feel like an obligation.** Avoid anything that is going to add unnecessary pressure to your life and take you away from your joy. I recently said no to being on the PTA and it was the right decision for me. I applaud the legends who said yes to this but for me (in the words of Marie Kondo) 'it sparks no joy'.

I encourage you to think about your own day-to-day for a moment and consider where your 'pockets of compassion' could fit into your schedule. See each one as a building block to strengthening your self-esteem, as brick by brick you tell your brain you're worth it until your confidence is so solid that nothing can tear it down.

Transitioning into 'Mum'

I think it'd be remiss of me to write a chapter about parenting and confidence without discussing the huge shift that all parents experience. This is the shift from person to parent, which can, of course, cause a ton of joy but can also create a severe loss of identity and a huge knock to our confidence as a result.

So why the knocking of our confidence? Well, suddenly your body changes (if you've given birth), your schedule is different, your home is potentially different (or at least full of tiny-person stuff now too), your social circle changes (usually) and your responsibilities change. When you become a parent there's not one aspect of your world that doesn't change but I think we're often woefully unprepared for this. Since I'm a mother, and it's birth mothers whose bodies undergo the physical changes both during pregnancy and post-partum, I'm now going to focus on motherhood.

In 1973, Dana Raphael, a medical anthropologist, gave this physical, psychological and emotional transition into motherhood a name to acknowledge the upheaval it brings: 'matrescence'. Very little research has been done into this transition still, and it's not a diagnostic or clinical term, but I'm pleased that it has at least been given its own title to signify the magnitude of the change experienced.

When you become a mother, you are suddenly expected by society to be fully focused on motherhood. There's an expectation of wanting nothing more, and while this may be the experience for some, many find themselves in an emotional tug of war as a new parent. In *Reproductive*, psychiatrist Alexandra Sacks' TED Talk, she discusses this 'push and pull' feeling in depth. The pull is that maternal desire to care and nurture but the push is the other aspects of our lives outside of this new role. The push to do the things we did before, the push to look the same and the push towards our identity outside of being a mum.

Nobody sits us down at any point and talks to us about what matrescence feels like. In fact, it can sometime feel like the world expects you to be the same as you were before, just with a baby on your hip. So many of us then try to attempt this. Until we eventually hit a brick wall and wonder: 'Who am I?' What do I even enjoy? What do I want? What did I do before all of this?'

Maybe you find you've lost that sense of identity because your world now revolves around your kids. Maybe you really feel you've lost a sense of freedom that you used to cherish. Or perhaps your identity used to be tied up in your job but you've cut back your hours to focus on your home life. Maybe your identity has been lost because you feel too busy or underconfident due to changes to your body to dress like yourself, or to do things that you once enjoyed.

It can be interesting to compare matrescence to puberty, which is another pivotal and transitional time in life when we grow and change significantly. However, unlike with matrescence, the support for the transition through puberty is provided as standard at school. We might have had to sit through an embarrassing lecture from a teacher or parent (or even both!), who talked us through the various teenage traits and stages we might be about to experience. I remember at primary school having to watch a video about puberty in class, sitting on the spiky carpet with my peers, staring up at the massive TV that had been wheeled into the room. As the cartoon images of the stages of puberty adorned the screen, we looked on in horror at the amount of hair that seemed to be appearing everywhere, as my teacher tried (and failed) to stifle his laughter at our reaction.

Although excruciating, the support provided to us through puberty helped prepare us for our transition into adulthood. This meant that when we struggled or faced challenges, we had the understanding and confidence that everything we were experiencing was normal.

This same support sadly isn't provided as we transition into motherhood, and as a result we can lose our sense of self and confidence along the way. So let's take some time to parent ourselves through this transition by having a go at the actionable points I've listed below. These are my favourite tips for ensuring parents no longer put their needs last on the list, and can be used in conjunction with the action points already scattered throughout this chapter.

From feeling unsure to feeling secure

To help you put into practice the techniques we've discussed in this chapter, here are some action points to get you started.

Inside:

1 **Identify your parenting values.** Take some time to think about the values that you hold dear, as a person and as a parent, and write them down. Put these somewhere you can refer to them easily (print them off, save them on your phone or write them in a notebook). Each time you get stuck on a parenting choice you can then refer to your values and ensure your choices align with what's important to you overall (this helps turn down the racket of other people's opinions too!). For a full list of values, see my website. If you need some useful prompts to get started though, here are some questions to consider: What were my parent's values? What are the values of someone I really respect? What would I like my family's priorities to be?

2 **Fifteen minutes of compassion.** Set aside 10–15 minutes at the end of each day, or perhaps once a week, to practise self-compassion. Start by considering the day that has just gone (and potentially some of the challenges that you faced). Then I want you to imagine someone you love and care about facing the same day

and how you might respond to them telling you about it. Next, get your pen and paper out and for the allotted time, I want you to write a compassionate response to your day, to yourself. Talk about yourself by using your name and with the kindness you'd offer to a friend.

3 **Drop the ball.** At the top of a piece of paper write 'Where can I drop the ball and let go of perfection, and how does this make me feel?' Set a timer for 10–15 minutes and free-write whatever comes to your mind (don't censor yourself). Once the time is up, choose three ways you will drop the ball this week and challenge yourself to make it happen.

4 **Explore and try something new** outside of being a parent at least once a month. This might be going to a music gig, taking a dance class or just scheduling 'adult-only time' (which sounds way sexier than I mean it to, although this is also a valid option). This can help to reboot your confidence that you exist as a human outside of the smaller humans.

Outside:

1 **'Slay' for a day.** I have no idea what this looks like for you, but I want you to dress the most 'you' that you can. If you're unsure what this means at this stage in your life, then it's time to play and have fun. Perhaps start by taking a nice shower and using the lovely hair mask someone got you at Christmas (that you still haven't got round to using). Could you paint your nails, take some time to do your hair, pop on the red lipstick that you used to love? Is it time to wear the top that still has the tags in it because no occasion has felt special enough to wear it? Today is the day! Or if your wardrobe just doesn't feel like this version of you any more, then perhaps it is time to treat yourself to a shopping trip and work out which clothes do. Be bold, be fun, be sexy, be flamboyant, dress for the version of you that you wish to be, even if you're still learning to embody this internally.

2 **Dorky dancing.** If we aren't careful, parenting can make us a little too serious. To counteract this horrid habit, I'm going to ask you to let down your guard, turn up the tunes and dance like no one is watching. I like to add this into my morning routine a few times a week (and it's something we do in The Happy Me Project community). Move your body, elevate your mood and lean into your most confident self.

3 **Shoulders back and chin up.** I want to see you leading the way for your kids by standing tall and raising your game as the powerful parent you are. You're doing great, so enter the room like you know this.

Guest advice

Anna Mathur
Author of *Raising a Happier Mother* (2023)
@annamathur

❮When you find yourself comparing, anchor yourself in what you know is true about who you are as a person and as a parent. Write down some truths to revert to when you feel wobbled by comparison. "I am loved by those who know me best. I am a good enough mother to my children."❯

#8

Job interviews

I have been rejected from about 158 jobs!

Perhaps that sounds terrible, and you might be thinking what kind of 'loser' has written this book, but let's look at this from a different perspective. This also means I've been brave enough to put myself forward at least 158 times (and many more because this doesn't include the jobs I *did* get).

The majority of these rejections were from acting roles. Actors typically interview – or audition – more times than the average person, so this level of interview experience stands me in good stead for this discussion. It allows me to understand the resilience and self-belief it takes to come back from the nos and the confidence it takes to show up and get those yeses. As a coach, interviews are now one of the areas that I work with my clients on the most and I love watching as their confidence soars.

Clients come to me so often for interview advice because interviews have an amazing ability to make our self-belief wobble and many of us struggle with them. There are many reasons for this, from the expectations we place on ourselves to the belief that a failure says something about who we are as people.

If you feel like this, you're totally normal. Fear of judgement and fear of failure are the most human things out there. But the good news is that there are steps we can take to alleviate the nerves and help us perform at our best. I'm going to share these with you now.

I've broken this chapter down into seven sections, so if you want to skip forward to a specific stage, you fly yourself over there now my friend. (We don't stand on ceremony in these parts and we're pretty lawless when it comes to the 'rules of reading'!). Here we go:

1. The preparation

2. The journey to the interview

3. The first impression

4. The interview

5. The nerves

6. The end of the interview

7. The outcome

1. The preparation

You've got an interview. Congratulations! Just getting one is a big deal so let's not underplay this accomplishment. You are awesome! Now it's time to prepare. To do this, I've split the preparation down into the four Rs: **Role**, **Research**, **Reflection** and **Rehearsal**. Let's work through each one in turn.

The role

First you need to make sure you know the role you're interviewing for inside and out. It might have been a little while since you submitted your initial application, so now is a good time to re-read the job description and remind yourself of what you wrote in your covering letter and CV.

As you familiarise yourself with your CV, begin breaking it down into three key areas to help you remember the main points relevant to this role:

1. Education and early career.

2. Big, important or significant jobs (noting key skills and 'wins' in this position).

3. The last role you did or your current job (again, noting any key transferrable skills).

As you re-read the job description, remind yourself again how your skills match up to the requirements. Have you done anything like this before or will this job require some training, for example? If you happen to know anyone with experience in the type of role you're applying for, drop them a message and see if they have any advice for you.

The research

Now you're clear on the role, you can start the research. In the interview, being able to discuss what's happening in the company and wider industry will give the impression that you care, you're prepared and that you'd go that extra mile. (And having as much information as possible as you enter the room will only help you feel more confident.)

The research stage is also a great time to be jotting down questions to ask at the end of the interview, such as 'It was great to see you picking up the [insert name of very prestigious award] last year, did this open up any new opportunities for you?' or 'It's exciting to see a second store opening in the city, is there a hope to expand further in the future?' Jot these down in a notebook as you go to save for later.

Research the people
Check out the leadership of the company. Who is in charge? Is it one person or a team? This information can usually be found in the 'About Us' section of the company's website. Some interviews will be with only one person, but often there will be a couple of people in the room and perhaps even a whole panel. If you want to feel as prepared

as possible then ask your contact for the names of the people who will be interviewing you. You can then look them up on the company website or LinkedIn and find out a little more about them. Do you have any similar interests, for example, or any contacts that overlap on LinkedIn? (The caveat, as always, is to do this research with a little care – you *do not* want to be accidentally liking their daughter's graduation photo on Instagram.)

Research the company

Learn what you can about what's going on at the company right now. Any recent wins or losses? Any big new hires? What is the company most proud of – what does it highlight on its website? Does it have any standout products or clients? Does the company operate globally with offices around the world or is it focused on one specific region?

Look at where the company sits within the wider industry. Is it a market leader? Or perhaps it's a start-up? Who is the company's main competition and how does the company try to differentiate itself from them? See what you can find about the company culture too. What's the working-from-home policy like? Do they have any sports teams you could join?

The reflection

Now you have the information about the role and the company, it's time to reflect on yourself.

Your strengths

When reflecting, it's easy for us to focus on the negatives about ourselves (and the negatives in life generally), as the brain is wired to look out for potential threats and danger (which we discuss in chapter 1). This means it is harder for the brain to seek out the positives about ourselves, but it's essential we do so (and turn the volume up!). We need to make sure we can talk confidently about our strengths. An interview is not the time to act humble or let self-doubt get loud.

'We need to make sure we can **talk confidently about our strengths**. An interview is <u>not</u> the time to act humble or let self-doubt get loud.'

A good way to practise this is to think back to times when you've done well at work. Have you had any particular high points and, if so, consider the skills you used to get there – perhaps it was decision making or leading a team. Think about any compliments you may have received from managers, and even take a look at old appraisals for any positive feedback. Have you done any qualifications that would be relevant, and don't forget about soft skills too, such as empathy, patience and time management.

Create a list of your strengths that are relevant to this role and then try using my three P system to prepare examples of how your strengths have led to success. Outline the **problem** (what needed to be fixed?), then explain the **plan** (what steps did you take to fix it and what strengths did you use during the process?) and what was the end **pay-off** (what was the result?). For example:

Strength 1: 'I speak three languages and this means I can support our customers who are non-English speakers.'

- **Problem:** We were missing out on valuable non-English-speaking customers because we didn't have anyone who spoke another language.
- **Plan:** I internally advertised that I speak three languages and I offered to support any of my colleagues trying to bring in new non-English-speaking customers.
- **Pay-off:** My language support meant more of my colleagues could target non-English-speaking customers and we increased our revenue.

Strength 2: 'I am extremely organised and in my last job I supported my manager in arranging a huge training event, where I was in charge of booking venues, the speakers and scheduling the day.'

- **Problem:** A very busy training event that required a lot of organising.

- **Plan:** I organised the event, using a brand-new system, making sure to keep everyone in the loop and ensure everyone knew where they were going and what they were doing.
- **Pay-off:** The event was a huge success, with attendees, speakers and management feeling very happy.

Strength 3: 'I am a confident leader and enjoy bringing a team together and utilising everyone's individual strengths. In my last role as team leader, my straightforward approach saw our team become the top sales team in the country.'

- **Problem:** My last team were rarely hitting sales targets and were very unmotivated.
- **Plan:** I created a supportive team environment with a focus on mini competitions and fun to help with morale.
- **Pay-off:** My team smashed their sales targets and had fun doing so.

Long term, it's a good idea to start taking note of when you have a work success or receive some praise. That way, you begin to build up a bank of 'things I'm good at' that can be opened in moments such as this. My wonderful editor shared that she keeps a folder of nice emails she receives, which is a fabulous idea!

Your weaknesses

No one enjoys this part of the interview. Who on earth wants to discuss what they're not so good at? It's important, though, for employers to see how self-aware and honest you are, plus it's a good way to test how you support yourself (so these weaknesses don't become a problem in a work context). The good news is that we can prepare beforehand and even run our answers by other people to check we haven't gone too far in our honesty.

What an employer doesn't need to hear:

- 'I don't have any weaknesses.' This shows a lack of self-awareness or dishonesty.
- 'I'm just such a perfectionist.' Cringe, no! This sounds like a 'fake' weakness and a (very overused) humble brag.
- 'Spanish men, chocolate eclairs and anyone who can play a musical instrument!' Avoid oversharing personal preferences or trying to be funny in a time that's meant to be serious. This approach is not going to make you look like a winning hire.

So, how do you prepare a good answer to this question? I suggest you look at past feedback or things that haven't gone well in your work and pick one area you struggle with. Then think about how you are currently working to overcome this, i.e. the support you have put in place to ensure it doesn't become a problem. Give specific examples where possible, such as in the examples below.

What an employer does want to hear:

- 'English isn't my first language. I'm more than happy to be corrected if I don't pronounce something correctly. However, I have regular English lessons and I'm getting better every month.'
- 'Presenting isn't something I'm naturally comfortable with but I'm keen to improve. In my last job, I volunteered to do two presentations to a group of 20 people and after each one I felt more confident. I am committed to volunteering for presentations rather than avoiding them so I can continue to get better at public speaking.'
- 'I tend to be direct, which can come across as blunt sometimes. In my last role, this was brought up to me by a colleague and it was something I hadn't been aware of previously. Since then, I've been working on being more mindful of my approach and I have seen my relationships with colleagues improve.'

Remember, talking about your weaknesses is not a time to talk badly about yourself. It's an opportunity to own any challenges you've faced and display self-awareness. The examples given demonstrate honesty and confidence and show that you're a problem solver who faces things head-on. And let's be real here, who wouldn't want to hire you?! You're fabulous!

The rehearsal

Lastly, it's time to rehearse. Search for common interview questions online or head to my website where I have listed some for you. Make sure you add any industry-specific interview questions to any generic interview questions you find, too. Then with your research and reflections to hand, it's time to rehearse.

Do this by writing out answers to all the common interview questions you've compiled and then practise saying them out loud. You also need to be able to talk through your CV – use the technique of splitting this into three areas as discussed on p. 206. I know practising out loud might make you squirm initially but trust me that squirming in the comfort of your own home is much easier than squirming in a job interview. So, squirm till you don't squirm any more and practise till you feel confident with your answers. Practice makes perfect, after all.

If you want to take it further, you could record yourself on your phone to watch your performance back. Or you could write your interview questions on flashcards and ask a trusted friend to do a practice interview with you, and provide supportive feedback.

During this practice stage, notice if your speech tends to become rapid. When we're nervous, we tend to speed up and get less comfortable with pauses. If this is you, see how it feels to go at half the speed and try bringing in some pauses too. It will feel uncomfortable at first but it's hugely worth practising. Pauses and slower talking imply confidence and authority (since we're happy to make the other person wait for our answer) compared to a nervous counterpart who is in a rush to fill every gap.

Many interviews are now online, so during the rehearsal period, remember to set up and practise with any technology you'll need. Record yourself, if possible, so you can see what you look like on screen and check that your eye contact (hint: look directly into the camera) and background is on point.

By writing out your answers and practising in this way, you're developing your own interview script, which you can fall back on in the interview room. In the real thing, these pre-prepared scripts can be invaluable because they help add an element of predictability to an unpredictable situation. You'll already potentially be nervous, so knowing you have a well-rehearsed script for common answers can give you a moment of respite and breathing space when they come up.

2. The journey to the interview

A friend of mine, Kate, shared a horrid story recently of heading into an interview. Kate was underprepared and running late. Such is sod's law, she hit every traffic light as she drove and the stress of this left her feeling anxious and short-tempered.

At some point on the journey, a white car cut in front of her, and Kate tooted her horn loudly. She then sped up to catch the culprit and indicated her fury by screaming out of the window and sticking up her middle finger.

In that moment, this behaviour felt cathartic, but as she walked into her interview she saw the driver of the white car in the hiring manager chair, and her heart sank. Needless to say, she did not get this job.

The lesson from this stomach-churning tale is that the interview starts when the journey begins. The minute you leave your house you might encounter someone who is involved in the interview process, so be mindful of this. It is also a good idea to ensure your journey to your interview is as calm as possible; you want to float into the interview serenely, not hurtle in like the cartoon-character Tasmanian devil.

So how can you use your journey to arrive ready to be your most confident self?

Well, first, I am a big fan of a trial run. This means doing the journey prior to your interview so that you alleviate any anxiety in terms of finding your way there. You can check out the parking situation, make sure you know the correct train or suss out whether there are any roadworks to avoid. Plus, if this could be your potential workplace, it's a good way to train your brain that this job is yours, and that the commute is going to be feasible should you get it.

For the journey itself, I've compiled a list of my favourite ideas below. As everyone's journeys will be different (car, bus, train, flight or on foot), some of the things I suggest may need to be tweaked depending on your individual circumstances, and some of the suggestions might need to take place before you leave the house. But I'll trust you'll piece them together in a way that suits you.

Travel idea one

Use this time to practise answering and asking questions out loud. Practise saying good morning to people out loud. I will say 'practise out loud' 5 billion times in this chapter (my literal friends, I am of course being silly, but I say it lot) because the only way to get confident with speaking is to speak.

If you're not travelling by car then the act of running through questions and answers in your mind is a fabulous top-up of the work that I know you will have already done at home. Also, why not try a firm favourite of mine, the 'fake phone call'? I use this as an opportunity to practise the things I need to say into my handset even though there's nobody on the other end. (Please do remember to turn your ringer off if you do this to avoid an embarrassing moment should it ring while you're 'mid-conversation'!)

Travel idea two

Now because you'll be speaking a lot in the interview, I encourage you to make like an actor or singer and warm up your voice. This can all be done before leaving the house or, if travelling by car, it can be done loudly and proudly as you drive.

Vocal warm-ups, tongue twisters, sticking on your favourite song (or rap) and getting stuck into car karaoke is a great use of your journey time. Your interview might likely be in the morning, and you may have had very little opportunity to talk yet, so using this time to warm up will give you the best chance of having the silky smooth and captivating voice of a winner. (What's more, singing can also be a fabulous tool in calming down the nervous system, so you might want to create a power playlist prior to interview day to inspire you to be your most energetic and impressive self.)

Travel idea three

As we bring attention to the nervous system, finding ways to calm and collect yourself at this opportunity will be time well spent, too. You can do this through listening to gentle music, spending time on a short meditation or focusing on relaxed breathing. (See p. 24 for more details on breathing techniques.)

Travel idea four

You could also use your travel time to visualise yourself either during the interview (and doing well!) or as if you have already been offered the role and are doing the job. Studies have shown that imagining something before doing it can support you in lowering your stress levels. One such study took novice surgeons and got them to imagine doing surgery, which resulted in them both self-reporting less stress and demonstrating less objective stress. As Buddha once said, 'With our thoughts we create our world.'

Online interviews

The four travel ideas above can all still be used prior to an online interview too. But I'd also add in here that your 'journey' to your online interview is mainly about prepping your space. I recommend that you:

- check the lighting (make it bright, face a window, perhaps invest in a ring light);
- do a quick tidy; interviewers don't want to see a pile of your underwear in the background;
- raise your laptop up so the interviewer isn't looking up your nose;
- make sure you aren't going to be disturbed – shut your pets out of the room, warn your children to be quiet and not to interrupt, and put your phone on silent;
- check the internet and your computer are working well in advance!

Once you've arrived – at the venue or in the online meeting – it's time to make an impression.

3. The first impression

'You don't get a second chance to make a first impression' is a saying you may well have heard and there is research to back this up. Let's take a look.

Studies conducted at Princeton University found that people make huge judgements about likeability, trustworthiness, competence, attractiveness and aggressiveness within just 1/10th of a second of meeting someone for the first time.

So that means that in roughly the same time as it takes to say 'hello' to someone, these conclusions are being made about us (and we are making them about others, too). The good news, though, is that even if certain conclusions are made, we actually do have a bit more time than that to affirm or disprove a person's initial thoughts.

A team of US researchers did a study that involved setting up interviews between 166 interviewers and nearly 700 undergraduate and masters students (who were all in the process of applying for real jobs). The interviews were 30 minutes long and the researchers were looking to see just how quickly the interviewers came to a definitive conclusion.

In 60 per cent of the interviews, the interviewer had made their decision about whether to hire the candidate or not within the first 15 minutes, while in only a tiny 4.9 per cent of the interviews was a decision made in the first minute.

Now while this may still seem a little daunting, we can also conclude that this means if we nail those first 15 minutes, we'll have to do something really crazy after this time to screw it up. I know that your inner critic just told some of you that you'll be the one who does screw it up, but let's silence this noise by running through the whole process so you can be full to the brim of interview confidence when it is time to make your first impression. Below is a list of things we can think about.

Smile

When walking into the interview space, make sure to recognise that anyone you meet needs to be greeted with your best self. The receptionist might be the son or daughter of the CEO. The person taking you to the interview room might have been tasked with feeding back their thoughts about you. You need to make sure that from the second you arrive you are portraying the version of you that will be getting this job.

A genuine smile is called a Duchenne smile. It is signalled by an upturned mouth, crinkled eyes and an authentic positive emotion. It's named after the French physician Guillaume Duchenne, who studied the muscles in the human body, including the ones that control facial expressions. One way he did this was by passing electrical currents through live subjects and then taking photos of their weirdly contorted faces (which doesn't sound horrifying at all, does it?!).

People used to believe that a genuine Duchenne smile couldn't be faked because it would always result in people looking phoney. However, it appears that around 80 per cent of us actually *can* fake a smile and make it look believable. Since smiling is one of the best ways to get people to like us, trust us and want to be around us, then a smile is a good tool to fire off in these initial encounters.

Body language

So, you're in the building, you've Duchenne-smiled your way through reception and now you find yourself sitting somewhere waiting to be taken to the interview room. This is not a time to get complacent and I want you to imagine the first thing someone collecting you will see. Think about this as if taking a mental snapshot from their perspective.

If they walk in to find you slumped in your chair, nervously turtling your body into the smallest version of yourself, chewing your nails or cradling your bag across your knee like a terrified child, it's likely not going to be the gold standard of first impressions.

Instead, we want you sitting upright on a chair, feet placed on the floor (legs crossed is also fine), your hands on show (placed on your knees or held just above your stomach if standing) and your bag placed on the floor. Your posture should appear open, with your face warm, relaxed and ready.

Use this time wisely to take in your surroundings, as this will help you to calm those nerves. It could also help you to gain valuable information to use later for potential questions.

Handshake

The time has come and the person you're meeting is there to greet you, so fire off that gorgeous grin and, if you're sitting, stand up. There will likely be a moment when a handshake happens (depending on what's culturally appropriate) and the general rule of thumb on shaking hands is as follows:

* Make sure your feet are planted firmly on the ground. When you're nervous, you might raise your back foot slightly into a sort of rocking motion (women tend to do this more, sometimes because of wearing heels and being knocked off-balance). Try to avoid this as it comes across as less confident than you might like.
* Don't grip too tightly, but remember that a limp handshake screams timidity. In fact, an Alabama University study that looked at handshakes found that they give away a lot about our personality type. Those with a firm, palm-to-palm handshake were found to be more extraverted, open to new experiences and less neurotic or shy than those with a limp handshake.
* Match their grip. If on a scale of one to 10 their grip is five and you have come in at eight, you're going to need to unclasp by 30 per cent, babe. According to *The Definitive Book of Body Language* (2017) by Allan and Barbara Pease, male hands can exert around twice the power of an average female hand, so be aware of this and adjust accordingly.
* One or two up-and-down shakes are more than enough and any more than three is awkward. I once met a millionaire owner of a sports team (not my usual crowd, I'll be honest) who nearly crushed my hand for a good minute and a half while looking me dead in the eyes without a break. This terrifying experience lives with me daily.

Small talk

On your way to the interview room, the small talk will ensue. This is a great opportunity to build some rapport before heading into the interview proper.

The person greeting you may be the first to speak, but if after two steps they haven't, that's your cue to talk. For the more introverted, you could utilise some of the info you've picked up as you've been waiting in reception (perhaps commenting on the lovely offices they have or thanking them for sending great instructions to get there).

Remember to keep the conversation light and steer clear of oversharing personal information. Now is not the time to talk about your 'nightmare' journey getting there, or how stressed you are that your gran is in hospital, or that you recently got over a fungal foot infection.

Online interviews

Interviews that are online won't involve the wait in reception, but body language, facial expressions and small talk are just as important online as they are in real life, so do be aware of these. The good news for interviewing online is that you can have a list of small talk ideas written down right next to you if you're particularly nervous.

In terms of body language, you may have to wait with your camera on until your host begins the meeting, so at this point it's important to remember your relaxed and open posture, just as if you were waiting in a physical reception. In fact, some body language can look worse on screen. Slouching, for example, will be magnified in such a tiny window so remember to sit up straight. I also encourage you to lift your hands so they can be seen when you're talking.

As the interview is now about to begin, the most important thing to do is breathe in, go in and give it your all.

4. The interview

Entering the room

As you enter the new space, you want the first impression to be that you are cool, calm and collected – a brilliant candidate whom they could see in the role. What you don't want is a fussy entrance that could risk you looking disorganised in the first few moments. To help with this, I would aim to only have one item with you in the room. For example, you might be able to hang a coat in reception and if you have a water bottle or notebook with you, be sure to keep them in your bag until you've settled yourself down in your seat and are able to get them out neatly.

Remember to smile, have your shoulders back and take a moment to give people eye contact as you take your seat. Place your hands on the table (if they can see your hands, and especially your thumbs, their brains are wired to trust you more, *see* p. 144) and breathe. You can do this.

Opening questions and pre-prepared scripts

The interviewer will likely start by easing you in gently with questions or phrases such as 'Tell me about yourself' or 'Why did you apply for the job?' At this point you can launch straight into your pre-planned answers for these (be mindful that these are relevant to the specific questions and not just a monologue presentation).

If you sense it's appropriate, you could offer to summarise your CV for the interviewer early on. This can be a helpful technique since by running through your pre-prepared CV script you're highlighting what you'd like to talk about, and hopefully the interviewer might pick up on these cues and ask more questions about the topics you've raised. This technique can be a gentle way of steering the course of the interview. If it works then it'll mean you're less likely to be thrown something from left field that you aren't expecting.

Answering difficult questions

Sadly, we can't predict *every* question that will come our way in an interview, so we have to be prepared to think on our feet too.

In fact, one of the things that comes up a lot when I'm coaching clients is answering difficult questions. They worry that if they don't have an answer then they'll have completely ruined their chances of getting the job, but it's OK to not know everything. You can still succeed. Your interviewer isn't necessarily looking for a genius; what they're looking for is somebody with common sense, knowledge in their particular field and, most importantly, someone with self-awareness and a willingness to grow.

A moment to pause

As we take a breath here, I want you to recognise the importance of pausing. The concept of pausing is actually very helpful for us in an interview setting too because when faced with challenging questions, it allows us a moment to collect our thoughts and deliver a more considered answer. Some of my favourite professional stalling tips (which can definitely be used in an interview setting) include:

* saying, 'That's a great question' or 'Thank you for asking, I'd love to explain more about that…';
* taking a sip of water while looking like you're thinking;
* saying, 'I just need a moment to think about that' and then taking the time you need;
* asking them to repeat the question.

Let me share with you a technique I was taught by Robin Roberts on what to do when you're *really* stuck for an answer. Roberts is a former senior partner at global consulting and leadership company, Egon Zehnder, and the founder of behavioural science consulting firm

Rehearse It! (that specialises in critical meetings), so he really knows his stuff. When faced with a difficult question, Roberts recommends:

1. The question happens.

2. Your brain sends out the warning alarm 'I don't know the answer!'

3. **You pause.**

4. You say, 'I don't know the answer to that question, but let me tell you how I would find out.'

5. **You pause again.** (Pausing makes you look like a thoughtful and calm person who considers things ... you look very wise!)

6. You then list around three separate ways you'd find the answer. You do this slowly, calmly and while breathing steadily. You also use your hands to confidently tell your story, such as counting on your fingers or miming putting information into three different buckets: one to the left, one to the centre and one to the right. You are in control.

Anticipate that if there are gaps in your CV, they may come up. If you've gone from one sector into a very different sector, this is also likely to be a discussion point. Preparing scripts for as many questions as you can limits the number of questions you'll find tricky.

5. The nerves

Statistically, recruiters will spend an average of 7.4 seconds looking at a CV and the hiring manager is likely to be as nervous (or more) than you as the candidate. Their job is on the line if they get the process wrong (which they very often do!). A recent study shared that a 'bad hire' (someone who is hired and doesn't end up doing a good job) on an annual salary of £42,000 can end up costing a company upwards of £132,000. Ouch!

The person interviewing you *wants* you to be the right person for the job. They want to tick the box to say they've found the perfect hire and message their work superiors to say it's done. So, before heading to your next interview, have this in mind: **you're not the only one who is nervous, and they want you to get the job.**

One of the biggest obstacles we face in interview-type situations is overcoming nerves. If this is something that rings true for you, know that you're not alone and we all experience nerves in some form. Let's look at how we can conquer them in the interview room.

Internal nerves – reframe your anxiety

The internal nerves are not something your interviewer will see, but I want you to have the tools to support yourself through this so you can feel as confident as possible. Preparation, creating scripts and rehearsing (as I have discussed already) are the best medicine for those internal nerves, but in this next section I want to give you a few extra reframing tricks to support you further.

Welcome your nerves into the room

I suggest that you begin by letting go of the idea that anxiety or nerves need to be eradicated. We need anxiety and there is power in its existence in the interview room. The anxiety you face has made you read this chapter, it will make you prepare for the interview, it will make you get dressed in your smartest outfit, and it will show you care. The person interviewing you knows that you are likely going to be nervous and, as mentioned above, they have their own nerves going on in these moments too.

Instead of expecting anxiety to wait in the car (or on the bus or train), it's much more realistic to instead put your arms around your anxiety, bring it into the interview room with you and learn to support yourself as you ride its waves. Anxiety isn't the enemy – it's natural – so reframing how you see nerves in this way is a great first step to feeling better.

Tell yourself you're excited

Anxiety displays in our bodies in a similar way to excitedness. Therefore, when you feel the nerves kick in, try telling yourself 'I'm excited' rather than 'I'm nervous.' This will help take your brain from a state of panic and fear to a more positive place where you are excited about the opportunities ahead of you. This can be something you say in your mind or at home in the form of an affirmation: 'I am excited about my job interview' or 'I'm excited to meet new people and show them what I know.' Give it a try and see how it feels for you.

> **'We need anxiety and there is power in its existence in the interview room.'**

Physical nerves – identify your tells

The external display of nerves is something that interviewers may pick up on, so try to manage some of these so you appear as confident as possible. A first step is noticing how anxiety shows up externally, and this will look different for everyone.

My own physical displays of nervousness are rubbing my neck and collarbone, a dry mouth, tense shoulders, shallow breathing and fiddling with jewellery (I'm giving all my secrets away here!). A lot of what we do with our physical selves, when we're nervous, revolves around self-soothing behaviour. This can have a calming effect on us internally but unfortunately, within the interview room, it can make us look unconfident and unprepared.

Take a moment now to think back to a time when you felt nervous – a job interview, exam or driving test, for example. Picture yourself there now. Imagine the room. Imagine the people. How did you feel? What did you do with your physical self? As you imagine this scene you might even notice you naturally start to feel nervous and display some of your nervous tells (i.e. the outward display of your internal nerves).

From here, read through the list of physical tells below and see if you can identify any of these in yourself.

'I don't want to be here' body language includes:

- struggling to maintain eye contact and looking away (some of my neurodivergent friends might find eye contact challenging, so don't get too caught up with this one if that's the case, or you may wish to warn the interviewer beforehand if it feels appropriate);
- facing your feet and/or body away from the interviewer;
- rushing your speech and not taking a moment to pause.

'Hide me' body language includes:

- shrinking yourself down;
- rolling your shoulders forward;
- rubbing your face, particularly your eyes;
- touching your mouth;
- hiding your hands (under the table or in your pockets, for example).

'Defensive' body language includes:

- having folded arms;
- being rigid and being unable to move.

'Submissive' body language includes:

- looking away or down;
- barely using your hands to talk;
- nodding too much;

- using a higher pitch than normal when you speak, or even (please God, no) 'baby talking' as a way to appear more agreeable – this could also include upward inflections at the end of sentences (*see* p. 92 for more on this).

'Self-soothing' body language includes:

- fiddling with rings, earrings, necklaces or hair;
- biting your mouth, fingers or nails;
- short, sharp breathing;
- cracking knuckles;
- wringing your hands;
- rubbing your arms;
- touching your neck;
- rubbing your ears;
- fidgeting and moving around a lot.

I have a horrible statistic for my fellow fidgety friends out there (and I include myself in this!). Adecco Staffing USA, a workforce solutions company, surveyed over 500 hiring managers and results showed that 26 per cent of applicants interviewed were rejected for fidgeting too much. From their perspective, the fidgeting showed a lack of confidence and preparedness. Now, of course, you and I know that isn't necessarily true, but in an interview situation it doesn't matter because we have a short amount of time to display a version of us that looks confident. Therefore, self-awareness and an understanding of our actions that might be perceived as unconfident is extremely important.

Learn how to support yourself

Can I share my own way of supporting my constant need to move?

I don't try to stop it (completely). I just redirect it to where it can't be seen. The secret weapon? Wiggling my toes. I am the epitome of the swan on the lake who can appear calm and serene on the surface, but underneath is kicking those legs wildly (or wiggling its toes as the case may be).

Here are a few other ideas you might want to play around with to support yourself:

- Dry throat? – Make sure to have a bottle of water in the room with you.
- Do you play with your hair? – Have your hair tied up and out of the way.
- Do you fiddle with jewellery? – It might be an idea to take it off for the interview.
- Do you have jittery nervous energy? – Would an early morning workout or doing something physical support you beforehand?
- Do you forget to show your hands when you're nervous? – Perhaps paint your nails so you'll feel like you want to show them off.
- Are you a panicky breather? – Get into a regular practice of slow and calm breathing, aiming to fill up your stomach by belly breathing (*see* p. 156) and slowing down your pace.
- Do you close off your body language when you're nervous? – When you're at home, practise expansive body language and when in the interview, try dropping your shoulders and releasing any tension with calm breathing.
- Are you a mouth and face toucher? – In the run-up to the interview, try to become aware of when you do this. Rather than telling your brain to stop (which it may well then reject and do more of it), try to see where you can divert yourself to (perhaps by writing something down or taking a quick drink of water).

What other ideas can you come up with?

If you feel anxiety rising during the interview, remember to fall back on the basics we've previously discussed. Take a moment to sip your glass of water, take a pause and breathe slowly, releasing the physical tensions in your body and helping you to feel like the confident, perfect candidate that I know you are.

6. The end of the interview

Final questions

The chances are that the interview will end with the age-old question of 'Do you have any questions for us?' and your answer will be an unequivocal 'Yes!' because, of course, you've done your research and prepped for this scenario in advance. Let's have a quick refresher though.

Questions you won't ask:

- 'How much holiday time do I get?'
- 'How long are the breaks?'
- 'What is the food in the canteen like?'

Questions you could ask:

- Specific questions about the company from your research stage.
- 'What do you enjoy about working here?'
- 'What are the main challenges I would face in this role and what would you like to see me bring to the table to support these?'
- Then, one of my favourites: 'In a year's time, if I had done a good job in this role, what would I have had to do?' (This is great because not only does it make you look conscientious, but it also forces the interviewer to imagine you in this role.)

Pleasantries at the end

One thing to remember when interviewing is that you want the interviewer to believe you have loved every second of this interview. You love being in their company and 'Gosh you just wish this could go on all day!'

This means that you shouldn't clock-watch, move around like you've had enough (or have somewhere better to be!), and you certainly don't want to scuttle out of the door quicker than Usain Bolt the second the interview ends.

The interview will likely wrap up with pleasantries and shaking hands. I read a funny consideration recently that reminded us to think about the backs of our shoes as we leave the interview room. This is the final thing that people will see and, if they're scuffed to bits, it's probably not the lasting impression you wish to leave.

After the interview

After leaving the interview I massively encourage you to do something nice for yourself. You deserve it! You've done what you needed to do and the outcome is out of your control. Interviews can feel so testing to our bodies and minds, so it's important to treat yourself. Maybe head home for a relaxing bath and to watch your favourite TV show, or perhaps take yourself on a solo coffee date or meet friends for lunch.

7. The outcome

If it's a yes

You got the job! I'm so proud of you and you should be proud of yourself. Getting a call or email to say it's a yes is a euphoric feeling and one I know you're going to experience (whether it's after the first job interview or the tenth).

If it's a no

Sometimes the answer will be a no and, of course, this doesn't feel good. However, a no isn't no forever, it's not a no for everything and it's not a no to you as a person. It may well just be no to you this day or no because the interviewer had more rapport with another candidate or they were a better fit.

Regardless of the outcome

Confidence in job interviews is about the confidence to believe that you *will* get the job or, at the very least, that you have *done the best that you can*.

I spoke to my dad recently, who was often in a position of hiring, and he shared that having been a man who came from nothing and worked his way up, he was much more likely to hire people who shared that similar proactive spirit. This is a reminder therefore that a no doesn't mean that you failed the interview or wouldn't have been able to do the job; a no can simply mean that you weren't the right fit at this time. There is so much more at play than we might initially see and it's time to move on and find the right opportunity for you. Because it is out there, trust me.

It's also important to remind yourself that you had the bottle to put yourself in this situation. That you were brave enough to take all the steps required to go through the interview process and put yourself out there. That's incredible.

Take time after your interview to acknowledge your wins (getting the interview, preparing well, presenting yourself as best you could). Notice the lessons from the interview – the things that worked and the things that didn't work quite as well (how could you improve on these for next time?) – and continue your quest.

Remember to:

- start talking about yourself like you're a winner already;
- see yourself in your mind's eye having already got the job;
- use positive affirmations that affirm who you are regardless of the outcome;

- practise and implement some 'calm your nervous system' techniques;
- keep going, try again and get back up.

Life is a numbers game a lot of the time and we're all just giving it our best shot. It's all we can ever do, so if you keep going then you're another step closer to your next win. Recognise that when you don't get something, this is often simply paving the way for you to get something even better in the long run.

Take some time now to delve into some actionable tools and make sure to keep me updated on social media (@iamhollymatthews) when you get that job or smash that interview (regardless of the outcome).

From interview stress to interview success

To help you put into practice the techniques we've discussed in this chapter, here are some action points to get you started.

Inside:

1 **Mental rehearsals.** Visualise and play out a positive outcome in your head and repeat it as much as possible. This is a powerful tool, so much so that research has shown that imagining 'exercising' does in fact build strength and muscle. A team of scientists at Cleveland Clinic foundation in Ohio researched whether we could increase our muscle strength by imagining doing exercises. Astonishingly, when getting people to imagine moving their fingers and biceps, they increased the real-life strength of their fingers by 35 per cent and their biceps by 13.5 per cent. Use these findings not to avoid the gym, but

to recognise how powerful visualisation can be and to spur you on to imagining yourself in a successful job interview.

2 **Write it out.** Before the interview, write a 'day in the life' journal entry imagining yourself looking back on the interview day. Detail how amazing the day of the interview was and even end it with you getting the call to say you secured the job. The caveat is that you write this in the third person: 'Holly woke up and was excited about her interview… She put down the phone and jumped for joy: she had the job and she started next month!' This technique will help you feel more in control and studies show that by talking about ourselves in this distanced way we naturally become more compassionate towards ourselves. If you then read your journal entry out loud you get extra brownie points.

3 **Use breathing to settle the nervous system.** Let's begin with 'voo' breathing. Breathe in fully and on the outbreath make a 'voooo' sound out of your mouth. Make it low and slow, feeling the vibrations in your chest and calming those nerves. Next up, try a double intake of breath. Breathe in fully through your nose, then go for one more quick inhale through your nose to fully fill your lungs. Hold for a count of four, then slowly sigh out on the outbreath. Do this a few times and you'll begin to notice a shift in your calmness levels.

Outside:

1 **Who are you talking to?** When we tell stories, we tailor the style to the person we are talking to. How we tell our toddler the story of *The Three Little Pigs* will not be how you share the latest gossip round the water cooler at work. To keep your interview script fresh, practise it out loud, imagining that you're talking to different people in different ways. Imagine that:

- you're telling a story to a child;
- you're sharing it with your 'naughtiest' friend;

- you're talking to a hard-of-hearing old person;
- it's a ghost story;
- it's a huge secret that no one is supposed to know;
- it's the most important information you've ever shared;
- you're a comedian;
- you're a wizard, witch or mystical being.

The point of this is to freshen up the way you speak, so that you can find different ways of making it interesting. It will also help you to remember your words and not take the whole process so seriously. (Feel free to send me a video of you doing it in the style of a wizard, purely for my own amusement: @iamhollymatthews)

2 **Jazz hands.** Practise using your hands to talk. Look for opportunities to practise a good handshake and when rehearsing your pre-prepared scripted answers, play around with different hand gestures to explain, add flavour and highlight your points. If you're more introverted and tend to prefer milder hand gestures, then I suggest you use big hand gestures while rehearsing.

For an added bit of fun, play a game of doing your script without sound and only using mime. See if you can get a friend to guess what on earth you're talking about. These techniques help to loosen up your habitual behaviours a little and you might even come up with different gestures that eventually make it into your final script (and, of course, it helps you have a little fun along the way!).

3 **Speak on it, girl!** Just like our body language, our vocal style can become stuck, stale and speedy, so let's mix it up and get you to see what else it can do. Choose either a few sentences or a full prepared answer to try out different ways of speaking:

- as low as you can possibly go;
- as slow as a snail;
- loudly;
- super speedily;

- in a gently timid voice;
- in the voice of someone in authority;
- with a different accent (I dare you to try doing mine!).

You may feel a little ridiculous doing all of these, but allow yourself to be in a playful mindset. In the 'silly' can be the shift that changes everything, so never underestimate the power of play.

Guest advice

Nerves and performance anxiety are completely normal. Remember, it's not about no anxiety, it's just about the flow of anxiety. I asked a couple of my performer friends about how nerves show up for them, and how they overcome them when faced with pressured situations.

Lee Brennan
Lead singer of 911, UK '90s boyband
@mrleebrennan

❝I try to *stay in the moment* rather than predicting what's ahead of me. If I think ahead, I can be very negative, like "I bet everyone will look at me and judge me." I now pull myself back into the moment with a bit of positive self-talk. Before I perform, I say, "Trust yourself. All is well. It's going to be a great gig!" The difference this makes is massive.❞

Laura White

Grammy-nominated singer-songwriter and former *X Factor* finalist
@officiallaurawhite

❝Preparation is key. If I go into a situation as prepared as possible, then I can be proud of myself and let go – I can give it to God or a "higher power". If I'm prepared, it's easier to face last-minute things that are thrown at me. I prepare mentally too. For me, that looks like going for a run and telling myself that I've just got to be the best I can be and that's all that matters (not impressing other people). I remind myself that it's not life and death, and I believe the right thing will always find you.❞

#9

Your appearance

I stared grimly at the slightly discoloured bathroom mirror. The smell of lavender and furniture polish filled the air and the sound of my family chatting in the next room created a sense of urgency. If I wanted to do this, the time was now. I picked up a razor blade and I brought it carefully up to my face. I took one last look at my bushy black monobrow and I marched forward with my plan. Operation 'thin out my eyebrows to look like Pamela Anderson' had begun.

Two hasty minutes later I bounded into the front room of my grandma's house with the confidence of a girl who felt solid about the choice she had just made. I was sporting two stubby, caterpillar-looking eyebrows, which were further apart than one might expect. As I took a seat on my grandma's recliner chair, I became aware of the horrified looks of my family. I felt the colour begin to drain from my face as my dad asked, 'What have you done to your eyebrows?'

This was the beginning of my teenage years and my experimentation with my appearance. Most of you reading this will have your own horror stories about something you did to 'improve' your appearance that you now regret (or look back on and laugh at) and I don't judge any one of them. We have been brought up in a society that teaches us that we aren't good enough and we need to 'fix' ourselves in ways that often have us looking ridiculous.

A gentle note here that if you are dealing with disordered eating or an eating disorder, this chapter may be sensitive to some and

I encourage you to seek the help of a mental health professional where appropriate.

Everywhere we turn there are beauty products we simply 'have' to have, ways to 'correct' flaws we didn't even know existed, and new rules about what is attractive. As a mum of two girls, who are always talking about the newest products, I am often shocked at what social media has taught them is 'wrong' with their appearance. This week I have been told that it's now essential to shave one's face and that the shape of one's hairline is incredibly important.

On top of this, we live in an era where we see our own faces more than ever. Profile pictures are a staple in our lives, whether it's social media, your company's website or dating apps. Plus many of us spend hours per week in online meetings for work, with a little image of ourselves firmly fixed on the screen. We're confronted with our own faces (and other people's) many times on a daily basis.

You might even find yourself popping a little filter on images of yourself, too, or selecting to soften the focus or adjust the lighting on video calls, all in the name of eliminating any 'flaws'. Unfortunately, this is a toxic habit (and no judgement here, I sometimes use filters, too) because the minute we glance at our real faces in the mirror, we can feel disappointed that we're not seeing the perfectly edited versions we portray online.

This phenomenon is even being dubbed 'Snapchat dysmorphia'. This has led to a rise in people taking filtered images of themselves to surgeons to get them to recreate the filtered 'look' in real life. Researchers at Boston University's dermatology department recently published an article in the *JAMA* medical journal stating: 'Now, it is not just celebrities propagating beauty standards: it is a classmate, a co-worker, or a friend. The pervasiveness of these filtered images can take a toll on one's self esteem and make one feel inadequate for not looking a certain way in the real world.'

We're also fed a confusing bunch of messages by society that has us believing we need to be so many different things at once. Look slim, but not too slim; have big boobs, but don't be so sexy; look healthy, but don't flaunt it; stay looking young, but don't look like you wear too much make-up; have womanly curves, but have washboard abs; make an effort, but don't look like you are. Um... What?!

When we see it written out like this it's no wonder so many of us struggle with having confidence in how we look. When we don't hit the current beauty standard, the impact on our self-esteem can be colossal. I am so bored of hating on myself and I detest seeing beautiful people like you hating on yourself, too. It's tiring, it's boring and enough is enough.

In this chapter we're going to work out why so many of us struggle with our appearance. We're going to touch on early memories and dig further into the impact of the media on us today (spoiler alert: it's not great news). I'll be interweaving many different techniques you can experiment with as you go to help you feel as good as possible. And a reminder, before we begin: this can be a challenging topic for many so do remember to take breaks as needed and be kind to yourself.

How early memories have made us feel

'Sticks and stones will break my bones but words will never hurt me' was a rhyme we were taught as a child as a rebuttal to use when someone said something mean. Only I didn't get it. I didn't agree with it. 'Words do hurt!' I remember thinking as a child, and little Holly wasn't wrong.

In fact, there's a body of research to show that words *can* change our brains both positively and negatively. A 2019 study from the

University of Jena in Germany looked at what would happen if participants were exposed to negative and pain-related words before and during medical procedures. They found that when patients were exposed to this language, they then felt the pain of the procedure more intensely than those who had heard neutral words. So, sure, perhaps words don't *break* our bones, but they can still hurt us.

We all remember words from the past about our appearance that have stung. I ask you to take a moment here to consider some of them now (and I appreciate this isn't easy, so I'm holding your hand tightly all the way!). Oftentimes, these harsh early words can be the root of where our insecurities come from, so they're worth thinking about.

Perhaps it was a passing comment from a thoughtless relative; maybe a mocking comment from someone on the school bus; or something insensitive said by an early partner. Perhaps the mean girls at school laughed about your acne/hair colour/eczema/mole/nose... The list of things people will find to attack us about is way too long to list here.

When you've identified some of these comments, begin to think about the impact they had on your life. Perhaps it was the first time you realised something about you was *different* to your peers or wasn't seen as pretty. How has it affected your behaviour or the way you see yourself in the world?

My good friend Shannon, who is naturally fair-skinned with red hair, has spent a small fortune on fake tanning and dying her hair after years of being bullied for her natural colouring. My client Emily still avoids wearing heels to this day after being teased for being 'too tall' at school. Another of my friends, Jackie, has dreaded opening the door for years without wearing make-up after cruel comments about her acne as a child.

I know rethinking this can be tough, so to help I'm also going to share my own memories and the impact these had on my behaviour. (Then we'll move on to working through these early comments, I promise!)

I vividly remember overhearing someone close to me saying that my sister was more 'naturally pretty' than me. As I eavesdropped on this conversation, I felt such a sense of shame fill my body that it was like my brain was reprogrammed. A seed was planted in my mind from that moment on that I would always need to 'try' to look pretty and my brain then sought out ways to prove my theory right.

> "Words and memories can really shape the fabric of who we are and **impact the levels of confidence** we take into adulthood."

I had always viewed my mum and sister as very beautiful (I still do). Growing up, they were both blonde with blue eyes while my dad, like me, had dark hair and green eyes. I had also noticed that princesses and Barbie dolls in the '90s (for the most part) had blonde hair and blue eyes. My childish mind worked out that this meant that I was like a boy and not pretty like my sister and mum.

I also grew up on TV as part of the main cast of *Byker Grove*, a popular UK show that at its height was averaging 5 million viewers per episode. This meant that millions of people saw my body going through puberty across their screens and, unsurprisingly, I found this a tad challenging.

Filming meant that for six months of the year, from the age of 11 until I was 18, I had make-up artists and costume designers commenting on my face and body as they curated the character I was portraying.

Over the years, I began talking about myself as if I were a product, as if my outside shell could be commented on like a handbag I was selling. (No judgement to my make-up artist and costume designer/dresser friends here, that was literally their job, but it's just worth noting my experience.) I found that I was constantly scrutinising and comparing myself to people I saw in magazines or on TV, and I slipped very firmly into something we call 'self-objectification'.

Self-objectification is where we view ourselves not only through our own eyes but as if looking at ourselves like an object, picking at ourselves and judging our every move. If you fall into this, it might look like constantly touching up your make-up, commenting on your body or adjusting your posture (after becoming aware that the position you're in might show your cellulite or the overhang of your stomach).

This type of 'correcting' is not only truly exhausting, but it means we spend our days punishing ourselves and seeing our bodies as the enemy. If this becomes our everyday norm then we start to take 'action' from this place, and might find ourselves withholding food, inflicting exercise as punishment, avoiding wearing certain clothes or refusing to do certain activities because the self-loathing is so loud.

My friend, if you're reading this and can relate to any of it, then I am so glad you're here. I want to let you know that you are so far from alone in this behaviour and I *am* you. I spent so many years listening to comments from others, hating myself and self-correcting. I was constantly looking for the next 'fix' that was going to make me look good on the outside and feel good on the inside, and I wouldn't leave the house without having performed an extensive (and exhausting) beauty regime.

What changed for me? I hit a wall.

I hit my low point and I was sick and tired of my own BS. I was sick of how much time I'd wasted in doubt, shame, fear and self-loathing. I wanted it to feel easier in my mind and I wanted to like myself. There was no giant epiphany moment; I had just had enough and I was tired. Can you relate? I bet you can.

Words and memories can really shape the fabric of who we are and impact the levels of confidence we take into adulthood. However, the good news here is that you and I have the ability to change our stories.

Unkind words are never about you

A good starting point is recognising that, ironically, the harsh words we're told about ourselves very rarely have anything to do with us. Unkind words are spoken by those with their own insecurities and problems, and the words are far more reflective of the speaker's issues than anything to do with us. They don't feel good about themselves and so they don't want others around them to feel good either.

A friend from my childhood was always telling me I looked 'too skinny' and making comments about my 'flat chest'. These made me feel awful at the time but now I see through adult eyes that she was struggling too. Her home life was chaotic and her mum was very critical about my friend's weight, so she was simply taking her feelings out on me, which probably made her feel better in the moment.

One of my clients, Helen, had someone in her life who always commented on her make-up. The person would present things as a weird back-handed compliment, saying Helen 'wore so much make-up' and asking, 'How did she find the time?' Helen said that years later this same person has now had so much plastic surgery that they are almost unrecognisable. I think it's fair to suggest that this person's words were due to how they were feeling about themself.

Perhaps you have a mum who tells you she was much slimmer than you when she was your age? But perhaps your mum now struggles with her weight so it's coming from a place of pain. Or perhaps there's a colleague who always talks negatively about your clothing choices, who happens to be going through a break-up.

Bad behaviour is not acceptable at all but this exercise can be helpful
to highlight that often painful comments aimed at us are not about
us at all. Don't mistake this as giving the culprits a free pass, of
course, because what they said was wrong. But understanding the
human flaws of the people who made the comments can perhaps
help you begin to let go of the belief that what they said held any
'truth' about you.

The power of positive words

Concentrating and meditating on positive thoughts, positive feelings
and positive outcomes is more powerful than any drug in changing
habits and beliefs we may hold within us. That's the conclusion of
Andrew Newberg and Mark Robert Waldman in their book *Words Can
Change Your Brain* (2013), which is based on brain scan research they
conducted.

The findings show that by changing the way we use language and
talk about past disturbing experiences, we can change where some
of these memories are stored in our brains or even eliminate them
(or their importance) altogether. This is helpful when we're thinking
about our own past experiences.

Based on this research, I have a lovely exercise for you to try:

1. Choose a time in the past when someone has said something
   derogatory about how you look.

2. Write down what happened and what was said. Then read it out loud.

3. Consider the language you've used. I suspect you'll find quite a few negative words in there. Now rewrite your story with the aim of shifting it to something lighter. To do this, try peppering the story with positive language, compassion, empathy and perhaps even some comedy thrown in for good measure.

I tried this exercise with a client of mine, Gemma. We decided to make a very negative experience of hers into something comical and like a children's bedtime story. The original memory was about a night out when her ex-partner had screamed at her that she was 'fat and ugly' in front of friends and she had been left feeling ashamed and embarrassed. When she rewrote this memory it went something like this:

> 'I looked over at this tiny man, who had turned as red as a strawberry and was hopping around the street like a kangaroo. As the warm summer night hugged me close, my beautiful friend Daisy stood near. She looked on at this silly, vexed strawberry man and shook her head because Daisy knew that the vexed strawberry was about to lose the best thing that had ever happened to him. Daisy felt pity for him. What a shame. The strawberry man did not feel good about himself as he looked on at my gorgeous body. So, the silly man sung out words like "fat" and "ugly" hoping that he would feel better about himself. His words didn't get close to me though, as the gentle wind took his anger and blew it back on to him. I sashayed away into the night (looking fabulous in pink) and left those words in his tiny hands.'

Gemma and I laughed at her new story as she read it out loud. She still reports today that when thinking of the event she is now more likely to smirk at our newly created version than feel the pain of the original.

4. Once you have written your new, positive story, take a moment to relax your mind and body. Take some calm and steady breaths (breathe in for a count of four, hold for seven, then breathe out for a count of eight). When you feel at your most relaxed, read the lighter and more positive version of your story out loud, taking away its potency. Repeat as often as necessary and maybe even share it with a trusted friend.

Repetition of positive words and language, rather than negative ones, can completely change how we view ourselves and the world we live in.

How social and mainstream media have made us feel

It's not only people who can influence how we feel about ourselves though, it's also the media. The information that we read, see on our TV screens and scroll past on our feeds has the ability to have a big impact on how we feel internally. Growing up in the '90s and early '00s, my generation was showered with *terrible* body image messaging.

Teen and gossip magazines printed photographs of women's bodies with 'circles of shame' drawn on them as they critiqued how they looked. Some of us watched make-over shows on TV, such as *What Not to Wear*, *The Biggest Loser* and *Fat Families,* where normal people were eviscerated for how they looked and ridiculed for 'flaws' they didn't even know people might have. This attitude in the media encouraged many of us to become hypercritical of other people and then, in turn, of ourselves. The damage to self-esteem was huge.

There is still a way to go (there is huge pressure on the contestants of dating reality shows, for example), but thankfully much gentler conversations about body image have emerged since those harsh days. It's comforting to me that when my children now see clips of the TV shows that we used to watch, they see it as unhinged and unkind.

However, we have seen the birth of social media. For every positive in life there is a negative, and for every negative there is a positive. Sure, we're kinder about our differences in many ways now and we definitely get to see different body types championed in the media, which is great. But our ability to leave a crappy comment on someone else's holiday snaps online or compare our bodies to other people's, 24 hours a day, is a less than positive add-on.

In this section, we're going to look at the messaging we receive from the media today, and what we can do to counteract the negative side of this.

> "Repetition of **positive words and language** can **completely change** how we view ourselves and the world we live in."

The body positivity movement

A phrase that has slipped into popular vernacular in relatively recent times is 'body positivity'. Since around 2012 there has been a rise in the modern-day body positivity movement on social media. This aims to be inclusive in its approach, challenging perceptions of weight, size and appearance to embrace all body types and fight against the beauty standards of the past. Sounds pretty good, right?

Body positivity as a movement actually started back in the 1960s when the phrase 'fat acceptance' came into our vocabulary. It was a time when the hourglass figure of the 1950s was no longer in fashion. Gone was the obsession with the big hips and big boobs of stars such as Marilyn Monroe and Elizabeth Taylor, and instead the Swinging Sixties brought with it a new body ideal in the form of models like Twiggy. An ultra-slim, androgenous physique was now on trend and a rise in eating disorders came with it. Once again, women were being told that in order for their bodies to be seen as attractive, they probably had to change them. This first wave of body positivity began as feminist women tried to reclaim the word 'fat' and stop it from being seen as a negative.

The modern social media revolution of body positivity began in the 2010s. It was started by voices in the LGBTQ+ community and from women of colour, such a Gabi Gregg (@gabifresh), Marie Denee (@mariedenee) and Brandee J (@brandeekurvyj), who believed that their body types were not being represented in the mainstream media. As a result, they began sharing their own stories on social media to elevate the voices of plus-size women. They kicked down doors that had once been closed to them by creating brands that represented plus-size women, and they empowered people with the notion that they didn't have to accept the unrealistic ideals of how physical attractiveness was traditionally presented.

These early campaigners had such an impact on social media that the concept of highlighting different body types and challenging the traditional standards of beauty was then picked up by big brands and the mainstream media. In 2017, the American women's underwear company Aerie launched their campaign '#AerieREAL, in which they promised not to retouch their models' cellulite, fat rolls or body hair. Today, this is much more commonplace but back then it was far from the norm.

As with most things though, body positivity breaking into the mainstream had both a positive and a negative impact. The original messaging often became lost as the marginalised groups whom the movement had sought to highlight in the beginning were still not always being the ones championed. Instead, slender white women often had their voices heard loudest.

The vulnerability we were beginning to see across social media was comforting to many. For some, this movement has been incredible and a fantastic way to start teaching women (and men) that our bodies are great as they are.

Work still needed

In recent years, however, the body positivity movement has been criticised for encouraging us to focus on how we look more than ever. One can feel pressure, for example, to love and embrace every part of yourself at all times. If you don't do this then you can be seen as, or made to feel like, a failure.

Body positivity has also been accused of promoting unhealthy attitudes towards weight and even, in some corners of the internet, been accused of being actively hostile to women who mention they might want to lose some weight or try to do so.

As a smaller-than-average woman, I have had people comment on my body and shame me for being petite (something I can't help) throughout my life. On one occasion I was invited to a 'body positive' lingerie fashion show and was excited to see an array of body types (and probably spent too much money on underwear!). The host opened with, 'Thank you for coming, you will see that the models we have tonight are *real* women and represent *real* women, none of those stick-thin size 6 models.' The audience loved it and cheered as I (and probably a few others too) sat there feeling like a figment of people's imaginations (not being 'real' an' all!). It highlighted to me that there was still work to be done on how we discuss the bodies we are in and inclusivity.

I may not understand the experience of the originators of the body positivity movement but I 100 per cent support their mission and believe we must challenge the status quo. If we are to get *real* about body positivity (while ensuring not to minimise the voices of those who started the revolution) then it means embracing *everyone*.

There's still much work to be done on this and we don't see enough diversity of race, disability and 'visible differences' in the mainstream media. Or, when we do, it can feel performative or that the messaging is still about people's exterior over who they are and what they're doing. This leaves many people still feeling like the way they look isn't acceptable.

The wonderful Laura Mathias (@relightalopecia) lost her hair at the age of 13 and has become a campaigner for Changing Faces (@changingfacesuk). This is a charity that supports those with marks, scars or conditions that mean people will often judge or comment on their physical appearance. Laura is very open about her own challenges with embracing her appearance and told me:

'Losing all my hair was a massive and unexpected change to my identity. I don't want to be ashamed of being bald any more. In fact, I don't want any person, whatever age, for whatever reason, to be ashamed of not having hair just because society has told us we should be. I want to see inspirational and real people on the catwalk, not aspirational and unattainable beauty. It's OK to feel like losing your hair is the worst thing to happen and want to hide it from the world. Equally, it's OK to embrace being bald or having fun with wigs. Your hair loss experience and how you deal with it is unique to you. The world will catch up and see how wearing "alternative hair" or having none really isn't a big deal.'

I recently tried to explain the concept of 'beauty standards' or what 'conventionally attractive' meant to my then nine-year-old daughter (I'm fun on the school run!). She looked at me like I had gone mad and said, 'But everyone likes different things, Mum. Not everyone thinks the same things are beautiful.' And there we have it: the truth out of the mouth of a child.

The reality is that trying to feel confident in our bodies is a communal experience and no one is immune. From the muscly man you spot on the beach to the women you see on social media from size 0 to size 24+ (and everything in between), we all have our struggles. We're all trying to navigate the world and the mixed messages we receive.

The best way to move forward, though, is to control what we can. And what we can control is this: how we personally feel about ourselves. So, let's take a look at this now.

'I'm ready to be nice to myself, where do I start?'

We start small. We start by taking mini daily actions towards stripping back the body image lies we've grown up with and we get there with compassion. Now I **love** a challenge and I know the competitive among you probably do, too, so I am going to set you three challenges to start with. These body image-boosting missions (should you choose to accept them) might just change your world for the better. Bold statement, I know, but have a go!

Challenge 1:

Changing your body image doesn't start with changing your physical appearance but with your thoughts. By changing your self-talk, you can begin changing how you feel. We hear the phrase 'seeing is believing' but when it comes to body image, we often have a skewed perception of what we look like (based on years of negative self-talk) and so 'saying is believing' feels like a far more actionable phrase. So...

For the next month, every time you hear yourself being negative about your appearance: STOP, NOTICE and then REPLACE it with three positive or neutral statements, such as 'I love my body because it allows me to get from A to B' or 'I like how strong my legs are.' You can (for extra points) write down whatever statement you replaced the negative with. This can be read at a later date to further embed the message. Pay particular attention to trigger events or times of the day when negative thoughts are more likely to slip in, such as getting out of the shower, trying on clothes in a changing room or heading to the beach.

Challenge 2:

Turn down the body comparison by filtering your feed. Unfollow 'trigger' accounts that ignite your inner critical voice (yep, all of 'em). Is it the cast of Love Island, the Kardashians or the hot girl from work? If it's causing you to turn on yourself, let's at least for now cut it out. Take 15 minutes to scroll through your social media and kick-start this habit by unfollowing some people.

When you do see someone you think has an enviable appearance, rather than using this as a stick to beat yourself with, see if you can appreciate them. Rather than seeing any difference between you and them as inherently negative, just view it as different. Then move on with your day.

Challenge 3:

Write a letter to your younger self. If you can find a picture, maybe of you in your awkward teenage years (or have you hidden all those photos?), then have it out as you work or even stick it to the letter.

Write this letter with your adult mind because I want you to see your younger self through these mature eyes. Be kind to your younger self, be understanding, appreciate how you felt and give yourself some words of wisdom for life.

This can be an emotional exercise to do and you might find you want to scoop your younger self out of that photograph and hug them tight. I would actively encourage you to imagine doing this. Younger you needed it . . . Going forward, as you hear yourself being critical of how you look, bring your mind back to the image of young you and know that they are still a part of you. When you're being cruel to yourself now you are also being cruel to your younger self, which feels much harder to do. This can therefore be a great tool to help you become more compassionate to yourself.

Neutral is the new positive

If 'loving yourself' feels too hard right now, then here's another concept that might be a good fit for you. It is similar to the body positivity that we discussed earlier, but it removes any of the pressure. Step forward 'body neutrality'. This idea is different in that it doesn't ask you to focus on *loving* your body but instead it asks you to focus on *accepting* it, i.e. noticing your body's abilities and what it has or does for you.

Body neutrality might look like:

* 'I accept where my body is right now.'
* 'My body is strong.'
* 'I am in a body.'
* 'My body is doing the best that it can.'
* 'My body gets me from A to B.'
* 'My body is a vehicle.'

To the untrained mind, some of these statements might seem a bit lacklustre. But for those who have spent a lifetime feeling shame about how they look, and lacking confidence in their bodies, then these statements are vastly more positive than anything they might have been saying before. Body neutrality encourages us to stop seeking perfection when it comes to how we look; it's the middle ground between hating your body or loving it.

Actress Jameela Jamil is an advocate of body neutrality and shared in *Glamour* magazine: 'I don't think about my body ever ... imagine just not thinking about your body. You're not hating it. You're not loving it. You're just a floating head. I'm a floating head wandering around the world.'

Anne Poirier is an intuitive eating coach and author of *The Body Joyful Revolution* (2021). She is championed as one of the first advocates of the body neutrality movement and describes it as: 'Body neutrality is shifting the way you see your body. It is changing the narrative when you look in the mirror. It is appreciating what it does for you every day. It is tuning into your strengths, being grateful you have a body to experience hugging your friends, or seeing the sun rise, encourage a colleague... The way you see your body, impacts the way you show up in the world.'

Many people in The Happy Me Project community adore this concept and, if it appeals to you too, then let's look at how we can bring some body neutrality into your life:

1. Take care of your body in the same way you might look after an object or space you own (but that you don't have the same triggering attachment to), such as your car or your home or your office desk.

2. Begin to notice how your body shows up for you every day, e.g. 'I ran to catch the bus today', 'I lifted my daughter up with ease', or 'My hands allowed me to French plait my sister's hair for her.'

Note these examples down and begin to make gratitude for how your body shows up for you part of your daily routine.

3. Write down what's important to you in your life and how your body might support this, such as 'I love nature and my legs support my long walks in the park.'

4. Drop 'body talk' from your conversations altogether (and this might mean putting boundaries in place with those around you too; for more on boundaries, see p. 96).

5. Wear clothes that feel good, eat food that nourishes you, move your body regularly, and listen to what your body needs.

In the powerful words of actress Emma Thompson (whom I recently met on the set of *Lorraine*, and who told me my first book, *The Happy Me Project*, looked great, which left me a gibbering and excited wreck): 'Don't waste your time, don't waste your life's purpose worrying about your body. This is your vessel, it's your house, it's where you live, there's no point judging it, absolutely no point.'

Feeling good about ourselves – the external stuff

In terms of feeling good about ourselves, it is important that we don't completely rule out the external or feel guilty for wanting to sometimes play around with this too, though. There is absolutely nothing wrong with tweaking your appearance. I am certainly not some weird puritan who will say we should all be make-up-free forever or plastic surgery is a sin. It's your body and it's your choice.

You want to tattoo a skull-and-crossbones across your neck? That is your choice. You want piercings hanging from every pierceable body part? You do you. You want to work out at the gym and get that six-pack, wear clothes that make you feel sexy or apply all the make-up known to man? Enjoy it all. And if you want to plump your lips and Botox your lines, it's absolutely your, and only your, choice.

My only caveat is that before you do anything to your body externally that is irreversible, I suggest you work on your mind first. Heal the painful stories, challenge your beliefs around body image, check the decision is yours and not for anyone else and then, at the end of it all, if you still want to get bigger boobs or bigger lips, then at least you know you've covered all the bases first.

If you don't do the internal work and go straight to surgery as a fix, then you may find that the list of 'fixes' is never-ending. You might find that even when you 'do the thing to fix the thing' it doesn't have the desired effect on how you feel about yourself.

We change and we grow and at 16 I could list every possible plastic surgery under the sun that I 'needed' to 'fix' myself, including taking my breasts up to four sizes bigger (which would quite honestly have made short little me topple over from the weight). I am so glad that I did the internal work first and didn't do what my unhealed younger self wanted.

A note on coping with external change

I wanted to put a note in here somewhere about change. Because change can be hard, and change when it comes to our bodies is no exception (and ultimately happens to all of us over time). I know many people in my own life who have found change challenging when it comes to their bodies or faces, whether this has come through pregnancy, after an accident or just through the natural process of ageing. If you can relate to this then you're not alone and you're not being silly or dramatic. You are allowed to find this stuff difficult.

The Losing Mumma blogger Chantelle Donnelly went viral in 2020 with her post sharing that she found her post-baby body 'disgusting'. She was very honest in talking about her appreciation for its hard work but that she didn't love the way it looked. Ellen Pompeo, the star of *Grey's Anatomy,* shared the 'mental gymnastics' she has had to do in order to deal with watching her face age over 16 seasons of the show, as she played Meredith Grey.

For me, I really struggled with my stretch marks after pregnancy. I found the change of not having them and then having them hard. It feels embarrassing to say this because it feels so minor in the grand scheme of life. When my husband had brain surgery and had a new whopping great scar across his head, we laughed at me for being so bothered by my stretch marks. I get how ridiculous it sounds but it doesn't change the feeling. I am so very lucky to have a body that was able to conceive and carry my children. But I can be incredibly grateful AND still not like my stretch marks. (I'm working on it!)

No one is immune, no matter what their background or success, when it comes to finding change a struggle at times. This might be the obvious physical changes or the hormonal changes (particularly in times like puberty or perimenopause) that can cause us to dip in confidence. It's human to find this hard, especially if your face and body have been a certain way for a while and now they're not. It makes sense that our brains might need time to adjust. We must keep reminding ourselves, though, that change doesn't equal worse, just different. Give yourself permission to get to know this new version of yourself (at a gentle pace).

As long as we treat ourselves with compassion, kindness and seek to love ourselves as much as we can then I think we're doing just great. Let's look now at some more ideas we can play around with to begin enjoying the skin we're in.

'As long as **we treat ourselves with compassion, kindness and seek to love ourselves** as much as we can then I think we're doing just great.'

From feeling unseen to feeling like a queen

To help you put into practice the techniques we've discussed in this chapter, here are some action points to get you started.

Inside:

1 **Write a list** of 10 things that are great about the way that you look right now. Yep, I know you probably just told me in slightly stronger words than 'dream on' that that's not going to happen, but give it a shot. Then every night before bed I want you to re-read the list, and then think about something about your appearance *that day* that was great. Maybe some days it's hard and you just about manage 'I like this one inch of skin on my left calf' but after some practice (and on your best day) I have faith you'll be shouting 'Damn I looked fine today!' I know this one is tricky, so no judging yourself; we start where we are.

2 **Stop asking permission.** Confident people don't ask for permission or validation when choosing what to wear. They choose an outfit that they like, they pop that outfit on and they live their best lives. My challenge is for you to stop asking, 'Does this look alright?' or 'What are you wearing?' because it only ever plants the seed of doubt. If you're feeling fancy and want to turn up in a gold lamé catsuit, you do that! If comfort is the name of the game and you're rocking your comfy jumper, but you're feeling great, then do that. Confidence is self-trust and we need to start building your trust in you.

3 **Unfilter your feed.** Challenge yourself to stop using filters or editing software on social media to 'tweak' yourself. When you post something without a filter for the first time, this may bring up feelings of comparison or fear of judgement, so here are two options to support yourself through this:

I. Get off your phone and get outside. Go do something joyful and move forward with your day without looking at your screen again for a while.

II. Head to accounts that challenge the narrative around body image. I recommend: @em_clarkson, @stylemesunday, @alexlight_ldn, @miss_sparrowlegs, @mynameisjessamyn, @love_disfigure and @the_feeding_of_the_fox.

Outside:

1 **Get rid** of weighing scales. Any of my clients who have scales in their house only ever end up weaponising them and using them to make themselves feel bad. It's terrifying how quickly we start using these things as a stick to beat ourselves with. I have clients who get on those scales every morning and it dictates how their whole day will go. How about we just remove them? (PS Mum, if you're wondering where yours are, I hid them in the back of your wardrobe after catching the girls – my daughters – discussing their weight!)

2 **Practise being kind** to your body. There are so many ways that you can practise this kindness, but some ideas that came up in my The Happy Me Project membership recently were: applying moisturiser (because it makes your skin *feel* nice, not to make it *look* better), self-massage, getting enough sleep, drinking water, eating nourishing foods, orgasming, showering or taking a bath, and wearing clothing that fits (regardless of what the label says!). I gift you with a brilliant quote from one of my members, Hannah Wood: 'The size of your knickers doesn't define you!' I think that's definitely a message we all need to hear.

3 **Have fun** with your appearance. See if you can practise getting to know your face and body in new ways. Change your style, change your haircut, play around with make-up (either wear it a bit more or go without for make-up-free days). This exercise is not about 'fixing' yourself. Instead it's about being creative and having fun without judgement. It's about allowing yourself space to experiment and enjoy the process. Imagine you are playing a new role each day and you get to dress up as your favourite popstar, a high-powered lawyer or even an Olympian. The end goal isn't to be some perfect version of yourself, just to bring the fun back and practise creativity over negativity.

4 **Try smiling.** Now before I make myself sound like a 50-year-old male builder on a construction site in the '90s shouting, 'Smile luv!' from a white van, there is research to back up this suggestion. Smiling can help us look more confident (plus it can also give us a high chance of success in job interviews and boost our immune systems). Give it a try today: smile at people and see how it goes.

Guest advice

Becky Hill
Brit-winning pop star
@BeckyHill

❝Be proud of your bodies! Celebrate yourselves! Show off your curves! Cover up for no one and be confident. It took me a long time to learn this and I wish I had role models like that growing up.❞

Letter to you

Well, my beautiful friend, you've only gone and finished the whole book, you brilliant human. Although, you may have just flicked straight to this bit (which I 100 per cent always do) and you may even be standing in a shop reading this, contemplating whether to buy it (I see you!). If that's you, run to the till and do it so we can hang out and I can help you believe in yourself.

Wherever you're at in terms of reading this book, the fact that you're here is fantastic. It tells me that you are on a journey to be the best version of yourself that you can be and that you're committed to working through some things along the way.

I am forever impressed by those who do self-development. I love your curious and inquisitive mind and your desire to grow and learn. When you're in this space, it's easy to imagine that everyone around us is doing this work (and we most definitely know a few people who really should be), but they're not. I hope you're congratulating yourself for making changes, being brave and filling yourself to the brim with knowledge to build your self-belief.

You see, it's all a process, a dance, a back-and-forth of learning, trying, messing up and then doing it all again. Growth is uncomfortable at times, and I'd love to say there's a moment when we stop and we've just gained all the knowledge we need to live a happy life, skipping off into the sunset as we do. I'm afraid that this pipe dream will never be anything more than that, but we're going to make sure we enjoy the dance anyway.

I still find it utterly mind-blowing that this is my second book and I'm now a fully-fledged author. Some of you will have bought the first book and you're here for the follow-up; some of you won't even know I had another book (go grab *The Happy Me Project: The no-nonsense guide to self-development* now, you'll love it!), and some of you might have been gifted this by a thoughtful friend. However you are here, I am thrilled to meet you and I already know you're my kind of people.

Is it weird that I really do feel like I'm talking to you as I write this? I feel like I've gotten to know my readers. So many of you message me across social media or share photos of you reading my books, so maybe I do. I especially like getting to go on holiday with you or holding your hand as you go through a tricky time. I want this book to be one you revisit and use regularly to support your daily adventures and I hope to be the companion who gently reminds you to be a little kinder to yourself today.

There is a caveat to you having this book though (and if you knew me before this book or have read this book front to back already, then you'll be well aware that I don't lay down the law very often, so the fact I'm doing it now shows it's important). The rule, the one thing I ask of you is this: make sure this book does not become 'shelf help' and that you take action and do the activities set out in here. I see you smirking, because you know that you have a ton of books like that already and this book is too pretty to be left 'unthumbed' on the shelf ('Nobody puts Baby in a corner!').

You want to be a confident badass? Then you've got to move that ass to do some of the work. That's the hardest bit, right? The good news is that you've already taken the first step by buying and reading this book, and from here you choose a chapter to start working on and you stride forwards confidently.

Let's fast-forward in our minds to a year from now when you've really pushed yourself to practise self-compassion and do things to build your confidence and self-belief. Think about all the wonderful things you'll have had to do just to get there and then all the brand-new doors that are suddenly open and available to you because of that.

I'm excited for you and I dare you to be brazen enough to stick two fingers up at the old stories that held you back and society's expectations of you that made you feel 'less than'. There is literally not a better version of you on this planet than you. You're glowing, fabulous, awesome and one-of-a-kind (and I'll fight anyone who says otherwise!).

I know that some of you reading this will be a little nervous about this journey and perhaps you're still worried that you'll fail at learning to be confident, but that's not possible. Things move, they change, and you do too. Challenge yourself, allow yourself the freedom to fail, and remind yourself that every confident person you know has days when they aren't so confident.

I wrote a book on self-belief and there will still be days when it evades me. Does that mean I don't know what I'm talking about or have failed 'confidence class'? No, of course not, it just means that I'm a human being, like you.

This is your fork in the road, your sign, your moment, and the nudge to be bigger than your fears and your chance to promise yourself you'll keep going towards the life you want (even when it gets a bit tough). It's your reminder to prioritise you and walk towards your next 'confidence win'.

Will it feel frustrating sometimes when it gets hard? Erm ... yep! Will there be tears of discomfort and cries of 'Ugh, why is it so hard being a grown-up?!' Without a doubt (and they're probably not all going to be mine). But will there be moments when you blow your own mind with the steps you take? Abso-flipping-lutley!

Now because I hate goodbyes and I also know that this process is a 'keep walking and keep learning' kinda gig, I'd like to invite you to join my membership community, The Happy Me Project. And because I believe in this space with my whole heart, I am even going to offer you a free month's membership to see what it's all about. To get that free month, head to www.iamhollymatthews. com/happymeprojectmembership and grab your code. (It feels like a secret society now, doesn't it? Ooh … I should get robes and a den, shouldn't I?!)

The membership is a space where I coach my members live and where you get regular access to classes, workbooks, video recordings, audios, incredible guest speakers, VIP tickets to in-person events, and a community that has your back and gives you a safe place to land.

As a coach, I have learned that we are far more able to move our butts towards the things we want and away from our bad habits when we have a community that's holding us accountable and celebrating when we win. The Happy Me Project has that ethos in bucketloads.

Regardless of when I see you next, you are now a fully-fledged member of my Happy Me Gang. An odd-bod band of square pegs, who give life a go and know that it's a big game in which sometimes we are ahead and sometimes we fall flat on our faces.

I'm proud of you and want you to remind yourself that from this point on you have told your brain that you are building your confidence, and every day you'll develop the tools to anchor in those feelings of self-worth. Your brain has now got the instructions and has heard you loud and clear.

Are you ready to drop the doubt and work it out?

In fact, let's just take one moment to STOP and address any doubt.

Place your hand on your heart, take a big breath in through your nose, hold for a count of four and then sigh out a loud sigh. As you sigh out, drop your shoulders and let go of any doubt that still sits in your system as you read these words:

'I can get that job, say that speech and pass that test.
I can find the love, make the friends and be my best.
I can raise my game, shoulders back and lift my chin.
I can start afresh and start to trust that I can win.
I can change, I can grow, any doubts I let go
I am **finding my confidence** and I'll go with the flow.'

And then breathe in excitement, curiosity and willingness to give it a go.

You've got this, my friend. Even when you feel like you 'don't got this', you do. So go out into the world today sharing the awesomeness that is you with all whom you meet.

Holly x

Acknowledgements

Wow, there are so many people I want to thank for getting me here and the worry of both forgetting someone or adding to my word count is hanging over me.

I won't name my whole family, but know I love you all dearly and your support is everything. Thank you for having my back, you bunch of legends.

To my friends both new and old for sticking by me when I forget everyone exists and for allowing me to be myself with you.

I'd like to thank the amazing team at Bloomsbury, notably Holly, Megan and Lucy who helped check my words, guide me, and keep me on the right track. I *literally* could not have done this without you. What a dream team!

My assistant Sapna and her team for keeping my social media afloat; Kayleigh Pope, photography superstar; and the Awesomesauce team for guiding my marketing and being on hand to offer their advice (even if I sometimes only pay for that advice with Diet Cokes and a smile).

To Jill and Sarah at the Intuitive Psychology Association who I did my recent diploma with and who have allowed me to learn new lessons that better me as a person and a coach.

Every single fabulous contributor to this book. Your wisdom, knowledge, and advice has added the spice, the flavour, and the colour I needed.

Thank you to every single person that follows me online, is part of *The Happy Me Project* membership, my 1:1 clients and those that have attended my events. Every like of a post, every share, every time I see you with my books, I am grateful beyond measure.

To everyone who has believed in me and championed me both near and far, even if I don't know about it.

And finally, (and most importantly) my daughters Brooke and Texas. You hilarious, beautiful and strong young girls. What a privilege it is to be your mum. We are a chaotic house of passionate humans but, man, it's a house full of love. My wish for you is that you become the most YOU that you can be, that you create a life you love and that you like the person you are. I will be there to hold your hands through it all and I am so proud of you.

Other resources

I believe there is nearly always more than one route to feeling good and getting support, so please find below my list of several amazing organisations doing important work that you might find useful.

The Samaritans
Call the free hotline at any time, from any phone: 116 123
https://www.samaritans.org

Mind
www.mind.org.uk

Where to find a therapist
www.counselling-directory.org.uk
www.psychotherapy.org.uk/find-a-therapist/

Beat
www.beateatingdisorders.org.uk

ADHD Foundation
https://www.adhdfoundation.org.uk/

The Happy Me Project

The Happy Me Project membership is an online membership where I deep dive into topics such as confidence and all things self-development, via video stream. You have a bank of pre-recorded videos, audios, meditations, and ways you can learn to find your most confident and happy self. You will connect with other members and find a 'safe space to land' when you need it most.

Head to www.iamhollymatthews.com to find out more.

I look forward to seeing you in there!

Also available by Holly Matthews

The Happy Me Project: The no-nonsense guide to self-development

Everyone can access happiness – it's a case of learning how.

Holly Matthews is on a mission to make your life better, and she's keeping it simple.

The Happy Me Project is 60 short chapters of straight-to-the-point advice, structured for our time-poor modern world, and packed with practical tips on ways to fill your life with more joy.

Available at **www.bloomsbury.com** or scan the QR code: